MANAG
HEAD A

SO YOU CAN

BECOME A GOOD MUSICIAN

The Psychology of Musical Competence

A Musician's Field-Guide for Performance and
Freedom from Performance Anxiety

RICHARD H. COX

Provost & Professor
Colorado School of Professional Psychology
Colorado Springs, Colorado

"A musician may suddenly reach a point at which pleasure in the technique of the art entirely falls away, and in
some moment of inspiration, he becomes the instrument through which music is played."
—Edwin Diller Starbuck

WIPF & STOCK · Eugene, Oregon

Resource Publications
A division of Wipf and Stock Publishers
199 W 8th Ave, Suite 3
Eugene, OR 97401

Managing Your Head and Body so You Can Become a Good Musician
The Psychology of Musical Competence: A Student Musician's
Field-Guide to Performance and Freedom from Performance Anxiety
By Cox, Richard H., MD, PhD
Copyright©2010 by Cox, Richard H., MD, PhD
ISBN 13: 978-1-60899-598-1
Publication date 1/31/2014
Previously published by Colorado School of Professional Psychology Press, 2010

THE COLORADO SCHOOL
Of
PROFESSIONAL PSYCHOLOGY PRESS

Editor-in Chief, Louis Hoffman, PhD
Assistant Editor-in Chief, James Oraker, PhD

TABLE OF CONTENTS

DEDICATION

This book is lovingly dedicated to Janet M. Helin, MMus, PhD, a dear friend for over thirty years; a piano virtuoso, a teacher *par excellence*, and an exemplary role model, who after a lifetime of musical dedication, passed away May 17, 2002. Dr. Helin was an inspiration to me personally, and every member of my family, as well as thousands of other students. She inspired not only her own daughter, who is now a Steinway concert pianist of renown, but also literally thousands of children and adults across the United States, to perform and to enjoy music. If that were not enough to make her truly extraordinary, she worked extensively with mentally challenged, autistic, and physically challenged children and adults, demonstrating to a doubting world that even persons with severe intellectual and physical challenges are capable of learning music, and enjoying performing for public audiences. Dr. Helin showed to all of us the value of music as therapy in the development of an enjoyable and productive life for, regardless of age, intellectual or physical ability. A cast of approximately twenty mentally and physically challenged persons, under her direction, produced a most remarkable production of "*Annie*" for standing room only and standing ovation audiences in the San Francisco Bay area. Few in the audience had dry eyes when they heard and saw what these students had accomplished under her direction and motivation, and their dedication and perseverance. Jan's skills were demonstratively effective in public schools, churches, private lessons, colleges and universities, and in specialty therapeutic settings. *Kainos,* the therapeutic community in which she produced "*Annie*", continues to thrive and serve mentally challenged adults to this day.

Jan embodied the holistic concept of music as presented in this book more than any other musician I have ever known. She brought many persons back into mental and physical health with her application of making music both inside oneself and in performing for others. This was particularly true in working with psychologically disturbed adolescents who were able to "hear" her through music when they were emotionally unable to accept help any other way. As an aging and physically ailing person she continued to carry an active schedule of therapeutic music teaching, and performed regularly until she was no longer physically able to do so. When she was no longer able to perform, teach, or even talk, I visited her and played excerpts from many types of music. Her face brightened up and her eyes beamed with musical joy as she recognized each piece! Music was her life, but even more so, her life was giving music to others. She was sought out by far more persons than she could teach, and by far more audiences than she could accommodate. Thank you Jan, for your consistent role model, challenge, and life of inspiration to us all, which will doubtless continue for many generations.

"Music must serve a purpose. It must be part of something larger than itself, a part of humanity."
–Pablo Casals

ABOUT THE COLORADO SCHOOL

OF

PROFESSIONAL PSYCHOLOGY PRESS

The Colorado School of Psychology Press is an educational arm of the Colorado School of Professional Psychology (COSPP) and is managed by a broadly representative editorial board. The Press publishes peer-reviewed academic works that are consonant with the mission of the school. COSPP is an accredited graduate school* offering Masters and Doctors degrees in psychology with concentrations in several applied areas such as clinical, psychosocial health, health psychology, pain management, spirituality and psychological health, and offers additional course work including forensic psychology, neuropsychology, and the arts. A major clinical training arm of COSPP is the Switzer Community Counseling Center which provides a broad spectrum of mental health services to the community. Other clinics include Pain Management and the Neurosciences. The Press and COSPP may be located at www.cospp.edu.

*COSPP, a private, independent, not-for-profit Graduate School is accredited by the Higher Learning Commission and a member of the North Central Association. The Higher Learning Commission, NCA: 312-263-0456

APPLAUSE FOR THIS BOOK

"We are fortunate to have Dr. Richard Cox serve as a guest lecturer each summer at the Interlochen Arts Camp. His book, *Managing Your Head and Body so You Can Become a Good Musician,* is an insightful 'must-read' for aspiring students, educators and performers alike. Dr. Cox masterfully weaves psychological and physiological concepts with the intent to provide artists the necessary skills to create unparalleled expression in music. It is a remarkable resource that every musician should not be without".
Dr. Michael Albaugh, Director of Music, Interlochen Center for the Arts

"During my 40+ years of teaching I had my students read two texts per year. Dr. Cox's book, without question, would have been first for every student. The connections he has made between playing a musical instrument well and living life to its fullest are of infinite value to the young mind, as well as the old. Congratulations and thank you".
Ronald J. Modell, Professor (Emeritus), Northern Illinois University; Principal Trumpet (retired), Dallas Symphony Orchestra, Clinician/Artist, Conn-Selmer, Inc.

"In his insightful book, Richard Cox, a master teacher, psychologist, physician, and musician, leads the reader to ponder his/her own role as a musician with a message. By emphasizing music as communication and expression, Cox presents many anecdotal vignettes and possible pathways through the maze of distractions associated with performance anxiety. A concise work, but abundant in wisdom, this is a 'must-read' for musicians or any other performer".
Dr. James T. Elswick, University of Missouri Conservatory of Music – Kansas City, MO.

"Dr. Cox is one of the few nationally known specialists who has worked clinically in the field of performance anxiety. His common sense, creative approach is inspirational to beginning and professional players alike. For that reason, The National Trumpet Competition is proud to host Dr. Cox as a frequent guest clinician".
Dr. Dennis Edelbrock, Director, National Trumpet Competition

"You, Sir, have a very excellent book. I enjoyed reading it very much; it honestly covers every aspect of performance. I congratulate you. I found it very helpful, even for myself. Thank you".
Prof. Frank J. Kaderabek, Principal Trumpet (Emeritus), Philadelphia Symphony Orchestra; Professor, Curtis Institute, Westchester University.

"It took me years to understand that a professional musician's physical health and psychological outlook play at least as big a role in achieving success as great chops and years of playing experience. Dr. Cox recognized this early on and cataloged all the important details in clear, practical, terms in his book, *Managing Your Head and Body so You Can Become a Good Musician*. His advice, if followed only in part, will improve your musicianship by an order of magnitude. This is a 'must-read' for any player who seeks to excel".

John Blount, United States Commodores (retired), recording artist and clinician

"Dr. Cox has crafted a manual full of 'truths' that speaks volumes to young musicians upon their initiation into the wonderful world of music-making. Utilizing his experience in psychology, theology and medicine, he underlines the importance of music in each of our lives and the rich benefits derived from musical study. Each 'lesson' and 'commandment' is a gem and when studied and applied will enrich the musical and personal life of any student. The given ideas will change and enhance the way a student thinks, and this is where the greatest strides will occur – in the mind! As a teacher and performer, I highly recommend this concise field guide as an important and indeed necessary, supplement to any young student's method books and solo materials".

Prof. Alan J. Hood, Professor (Trumpet) Lamont School of Music, University of Denver, Artist/Clinician, Conn-Selmer, Inc.

ACKNOWLEDGEMENTS

This book was written as the result of a suggestion from Dr. Dennis Edlebrock, Founder and Executive Director of the National Trumpet Competition, that I have a "handout" for my master-class/clinic at a National Trumpet Competition Annual Convention. Since I was unable to put what I wanted to say into a couple of pages, the "handout" grew and this is the result. The list of persons that I, or for that matter any musician, must acknowledge is entirely too long for this or any book. My list would become a book in and of itself. However, there are some individuals that it simply would not be right to exclude in even the briefest listing. As with any musician, it is important to include my family and others who have endured the countless hours of practice!

I continue to be grateful for my wife, Betty Lou, who continues today, as she has from our high school days, to encourage me, as did her mother when I was a teen-ager. They presented me with a C.G. Conn (Victor 80-A) cornet upon graduation from high school, which is still in mint condition and that I play to this day. I never imagined that much later in life I would become a C.G. Conn clinician/artist! I must also extend a special "thank you" to our three now-grown children. All three of them, as well as my wife, are able to play an instrument and enjoy music. Jan Helin, to whom this book is dedicated, challenged me after I had abandoned the trumpet for nearly ten years, to play the *Messiah* for a Christmas performance on the North Shore of Chicago. I resisted, but she won. I practiced painfully to get my "chops" back, played the Oratorio (on a Bb instrument!–The Conn Victor 80 a high school graduation gift) and I kept on playing. She and her husband Rudy cannot be forgotten.

Others who must be mentioned are Wesley Hanson, one of my best instructors, who played a euphonium like I had never heard before, as well as Renold Schilke, professional trumpet maker and trumpeter for the Chicago Symphony Orchestra, who custom-made one of my B-flat trumpets and taught me so many things. Dr. James Elswick, and Dr. Dennis Edelbrock, Professors Ron Modell, Frank Kaderabek, Alan Hood, John Blount, Fred Powell of Conn-Selmer, Inc., Dr. Michael Davison, Dr. and Mrs. Humbert at Eureka College who taught me so much about keyboard, pipe-organ, and the real meaning of making music, and so many others who were both teachers/mentors of mine and musicians *extraordinaire*, continue to be especially important in my musical world. Then there were those who attempted to teach me to sing (with such dismal results!), but insisted that I learn solfeggio, as well as the keyboard, chords and transposition, which I came to realize are essential in the armamentarium of every musician. Others who cannot be forgotten are mentioned in the Prelude of this book. Especially in my gratitude are those who have graciously endorsed this book, many who asked if they might do so! As for the many others that I have not included due to space and memory, I ask their indulgence and say a huge "thank you" for what you taught me.

"Music is a discipline, and a mistress of order and good manners, she makes the people milder and gentler, more moral and more reasonable"–Martin Luther

"Canned music is like audible wallpaper."–Alistair Cooke

PRELUDE

My musical journey began at approximately age eight when I was less than a happy schoolchild. There were many reasons for my discontent; however, most of them are not pertinent to this writing. I was bored, seriously "hard of hearing" (now called "hearing impaired"), possessing poor eyesight, and among other things, I thought I was really quite dumb. The men in my family were carpenters, bricklayers, railroad employees, and common laborers, and I had been thoroughly indoctrinated in the necessity of "learning a trade". My father had a fourth grade education, my mother a sixth. I thought that only very smart and wealthy people went to high school and college, and there was no doubt in my mind that I was not one of them, and my school performance certainly proved it.

When I was about ten years old, I learned of a job opening at the local fiddle shop. The shop owner, a German fiddle-maker and master-craftsman was Raleigh Garrett. I don't remember how I came to know about the job, but I remember so well the first day I met him. He impressed me as a person that "knew what it was all about". I somehow think that Orville Hayes who conducted our little church orchestra, told my dad about the job. My dad took me to meet Mr. Garrett, and I remember Mr. Garrett telling me in front of my dad, as he handed me a much too-big denim apron, "Son, I don't know what you can do but I know you can learn". Earning a dollar a week and music lessons I did learn more than I ever thought I could. I learned to take dents out of brass instruments, repair fiddles and other stringed instruments, replace pads in reed instruments, and hand rub and polish both wood and brass instruments until my fingers were sore.

In our little church orchestra led by Mr. Hayes, along with Mr. Garrett's teaching, I was introduced to the marvelous world of instrumental music. Whoever showed up at our little church with an instrument played in Mr. Hayes' orchestra. Encouragement abounded and I never remember being reprimanded for the many mistakes and sour notes I played! I even remember the congregation being grateful as we struggled to develop our talents. I was trying to learn to play on a cheap, beat up trumpet. As I recall, we got the trumpet at a pawnshop down on the levee with help from my Grandfather in exchange for my doing yard work. Although I got the trumpet, I am quite sure that Grandpa never got his full share of yard work. The trumpet did not have a case and I remember my mother sewing a flannel bag for me to carry it in (the kids didn't realize that they were laughing at one of the first and most creative "gig-bags" -- imagine if she had only patented it!). Mr. Garrett was a good "all around musician", and seemed to know how to play every instrument. I had taken a few piano lessons offered by some social services program, the name of which I cannot remember. That was during the depression years and our family was part of the "public works" programs, "relief services" (today known as "welfare") and other government assisted projects, one of which sponsored music lessons for those "on welfare". Since we did not have a piano in our home at that time, I had to practice on a cardboard piano keyboard and didn't much like it. Although I did not like it, that "handicap" turned out to be a tremendous blessing. I have been seriously hearing-challenged from birth and I learned very quickly that if you cannot "hear" the note or chord in your head, you will not be able to play it correctly on an instrument. "Listening" to that soundless music as I practiced on the cardboard keyboard was invaluable and has served me well as a musician. Although I continued to study piano and pipe-organ on and off throughout my life, once I got a trumpet in my hands it felt "right" and somehow it was connected to me and I to it!

Understandably, Mr. Garrett, became an extremely important person in my personal and musical development and although as an adult I had moved far from my hometown, I visited him every time I went back to that town, Decatur, Illinois, until he died. None of us should ever take for granted the influence of those who give us direction in our youth. Thank you, Raleigh Garrett, Orville Hayes, my grandfather, my dad, my mother, my wife and children, and so many others!

Music became the lubrication of my life. I could lose myself in it. I could express myself with that trumpet and "say things" that I could not say to anyone or express in any other way or in any other place. Later in life music became a major part of changing my world from one of academic failure to a life-long student. Music was the primary happiness of my childhood and adolescence, took me on world concert travels, paid for some of my education, and brought untold rewards into my life.

I learned that an instrument and a person can bond – they can become one. The musician and his/her instrument often seem inseparable. I have noticed that it is very difficult for musicians to sell their instruments even when they get brand new ones. It is like giving up part of yourself to sell an old instrument that has become your friend. So trumpeters collect trumpets, and believe it or not, many pianists still have the piano they learned on as a child as well as others.

Music can become part of your life only to the extent to which you allow your life to become music. Music, after all, is the controlled regulation of sound and without such control sound would only be noise. A finely tuned personal life is one of control, balance, modulation, moderation, and the ability to meld the many themes of our life together into a continuous meaningful, harmonious composition. Life and music are in many ways exactly alike. Life is like music. We develop themes, arouse chords and discord, and observe the tension and struggle for dominance, then the enjoyment of the anticipated resolution. What you learn in music is far more than notes and instrumental techniques. The lessons carry over into caring relationships, logical and sequential thinking, styles of personal behavior, and literally "keep in you in tune" with what is going on around you. You learn to "listen" and "hear" many things that others seem not to notice. You see and hear discord quickly. You see the relationship between people and in all kinds of happenings. The wonderful results of having studied music go on and on. Even if you do not become a "professional" musician you learn to become accomplished and recognize, respect, and deeply appreciate the work and devotion it takes to become good at anything. We all must become "professional" in living life. Studying music will help you to do that! Playing an instrument requires that you learn to take risks – the risk of making mistakes- accepting failures – risking to perform in front of peers, superiors, and critics, as a necessary part of the path to success. You learn to happily accept criticism from others and criticize yourself constructively. You learn to accept the fact that success in any field requires much hard work and that music is no exception. While many persons equate playing a musical instrument to some sort of recreation, you realize that they are sorely mistaken if performing is a serious goal. You learn that music is a central core to your life and that a harmonious life requires the controlled regulation of joy, sorrow, successes and failures, and the stress of life itself, and without such regulation everything becomes distress!

Richard H. Cox
Colorado Springs, CO
January 2006

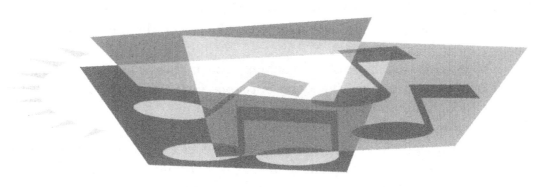

"Don't play the saxophone. Let it play you." – Charlie Parker

OVERTURE

Ronald J. Modell,

Music Professor and Trumpet Artist

Is there such a thing as the perfect mouthpiece that will do everything you desire? Is there such a thing as a perfect book on how to become a good musician? For me the answer is yes on the book, and I don't know about the mouthpiece, at least I haven't found one yet.

When I was ten years old my Uncle Milton Davidson, who at that time was first trumpet with the Ballet Russe de Monte Carlo, and two years later would become principal trumpet with the Dallas Symphony under Antal Dorati, took me to the Bach trumpet factory in Mount Vernon, New York. There a man came out and spread a black piece of velour cloth which he then covered with 30 or 40 different mouthpieces. My uncle said try them out, and when you find one that really <u>feels</u> <u>good</u>, that's the one we will take. I chose a 7B, and played it over 20 years. It is now 60 years later and I've only played three different mouthpieces, a 1-1/2B and now a 3B.

With more than 45 years of teaching, I have always felt it important for my students to read as many books on brass playing as possible, feeling that if only one thought in a book could make it easier to play, it was worth the time, effort, and cost.

A few years ago at an International Trumpet Guild conference held in Purchase, N. Y., I became acquainted with a wonderfully gifted man who was not a full-time professional player or teacher, but rather a lover and admirer of those of us in the wonderful world of trumpet. Though his love of the trumpet and music has kept him involved in both for much of his life, it is all his other life experiences which have allowed him to author what I consider the number one book on how to become "A Good Musician."

Dr. Cox has been blessed with a great gift of relating to his readers all the different aspects, both mental and physical, that are required to reach the height of one's own performance. In addition, and more importantly, to reach the peaceful mind set of acceptance of who we are in relationship to our performance, whether we are amateurs, part-time players, or full-time professionals. On the chapter entitled, "Ten Commandments for the Musician," Dr. Cox has given in 12 pages what takes some people a lifetime to figure out. I particularly like number six because I ask myself, how would Yo Yo Ma have done on the trumpet? How would Bud Herseth have done on the cello? Having the correct instrument selected for you is one of the most critical areas of success or failure. What truly amazes me in this book is that in just a few pages you can learn: "Managing your head and body so you can become A Good Musician."

Ron Modell
Professor Emeritus – Northern Illinois University
Principal Trumpet (retired) Dallas Symphony Orchestra
Conn-Selmer Artist/Clinician

INTRODUCING....................

INTRODUCTION

Learning to play an instrument is not enough to become a good musician. Becoming a good musician and eventually becoming a professional performer requires a combination of many attitudes, skills, and abilities that are not necessarily musical in nature. Learning to play an instrument, even very well, is not enough by itself. Only if you are able to put fine musicianship and good performing together can you successfully become a musician performer. There are thousands of very well trained technicians on their chosen instrument, but who do not have control over their own mind and body, and will therefore never become good musicians. Further, there are many fine instrumental technicians who are able to produce notes but not music. I recall the conductor of a symphony telling her audience, while congratulating her guest artist, that although she had been a music major in college (and obviously a very fine one at that), he "taught me to make music". She was helping the audience to know that there is much more to making music than playing an instrument well. Making music is also far more than playing every note correctly. One of the finest workshops I know of is presented by Ron Modell entitled "Making Music." Prof. Modell, (or "The Mode" as his friends affectionally call him), is the author of *"Overture"* in this book and a master musician and internationally respected trumpet artist. He emphasizes the necessity of turning "those little black marks on white pages into beautiful sounds that send a message". Music does not come from an instrument. It comes from deep within the soul of the musician and is amplified through strings, reeds, keyboards, brass, and wood that have become part of the musician.

Then, of course, there are fine musicians who certainly can make great music, but are themselves less than enviable as human beings. Throwing things, cursing, making unreasonable demands, arrogance, and egotistical behavior demeans the very music they make. However that kind of behavior does make for great conversation at music conventions where fellow musicians joke, ridicule, and otherwise castigate the "great musicians" who are in reality so very small as human beings!

Your head and your body are essential parts of your musical instrument. An instrument is an extension of *you.* It must become an actual extension of your body. The fingers of the pianist's hands are part of the piano and the piano is part of the pianist's hands. Some piano artists feel so keenly about this that they actually have their own concert-size grand piano shipped wherever they are performing. The trumpet is an extension of the trumpeter's lips, fingers, and whole body. The drummer, pianist, harpist and the pipe organ player are particularly illustrative of this point. These instrumentalists must use both of their feet and both hands as well as their eyes, ears and brains. I have always been particularly in awe of fine pipe-organists, having tried my own patience with that complicated instrument as well. It seems that there is no end to the things to which they must attend with their hands, eyes, and feet. It would appear that the designers of pipe organs try as hard as they can to build instruments that challenge human physical capability and cry for more hands and feet!

Careful observation will reveal that the musician fully engrossed with his/her instrument literally becomes one with that instrument. Those who "play instruments" but don't become deeply involved with it are not able to produce music from the heart. I recently observed a double-bass player who so well demonstrated quite by habit his deep emotional and bodily attachment to his instrument. As he played, he swayed with that oversized violin, he "danced" with it and "caressed" it, and there was no doubt that it was part of him and that he was part of that big fiddle. Singers appear to be different because the voice is literally part of the body. It is easy for us to understand that the singer's voice is part of them. Their voice is their instrument. In spite of the fact that other instruments are not part of the body, in no lesser way should the instrumentalist consider an oboe, trumpet, drums, or any other instrument to be anything other than part of their very person. To do so is to play *on* an instrument, rather than to allow the instrument to help you deliver your musical message.

Children are most frequently introduced to a musical instrument as "something they will learn to play". As a result, it is seen as an object, not as an extension of the self. Children who are introduced to the violin at a very young age are sometimes fortunately able to "grow" with their instrument, literally making it part of themselves, particularly when they are introduced to violins of increasing size in accordance with their own bodily growth. With most other instruments a small child is presented with an "adult size" instrument. Think for a moment about the youngster whose feet do not touch the floor, whose fingers cannot reach an octave, and whose eyes are not high enough to see the music holder, attempting to learn to play the piano. It is marvelous that so many learn to play in spite of these "handicaps". When they do learn to play, it is my opinion that these persons learn to make the piano an extension of themselves, and see themselves *"playing the piano"*, not "playing *on* the piano".

Managing one's head and body is a combination of conscious, deliberate, practiced habits. These habits can be learned. These habits can be taught. However, they do not come naturally to most students. Further, all too many teachers assume that the habits will develop naturally as the student progresses in musical and technical ability. This is not so. These habits must be consciously taught and modeled. Teachers who teach "playing an instrument" rather than teaching the habits of good musicianship that allow for life-long musical enjoyment and performance, are a disappointment to the profession. Likewise, good teachers model fine habits of living and musicianship. The wise individual does not study with a teacher who has become sloppy in personal thinking, or the habits of life. The wise parent will seek a teacher for their child who models a life style and professional attitude that they want their child to emulate.

When our habits finally are present without thinking about them, they only remain that way by constant practice and conscious determination. That which is unconscious must first be conscious. You must take charge of what you put into your brain. You are the only one that can fully *manage* your head and body. It takes daily perseverance and deliberate practice. And further, if you do not develop your own habit control, other people will do it for you. Who are those who will control you if you don't control yourself? Everyone you can think of. Those who envy you, those who wish to discourage you, those who want your time rather than giving it to practice, those who are ignorant of the dedication it takes to become a musician, therefore rob you of determination with no evil intention at all. You may have learned "stage-fright", or it may be your parents or teachers that cause you to have a loss of self-confidence, or other negative thinking. Since *someone* will definitely manage your head and body it's far better that it be *you*!

A balanced life must of necessity integrate the physical, the emotional, and the spiritual aspects of human existence. Good physical health, good mental health and good spiritual health results in prosperity of self and soul which is more important than financial wealth – although sometimes it results in that too! To gain physical, emotional and spiritual health one must learn and practice good habits every day. Someone has said, "we are what we eat". Although that statement is doubtlessly in part true, it does not go far enough. We are what we eat, what we think, and what we value. Good habits, however, do not simply descend on us from out of the blue. They must be taught, sought and diligently practiced on a daily basis. It seems that we must deliberately and consciously attend to the good habits on a daily basis in order to overcome the destructive ones.

Regular physical exercise, healthy eating habits, restful and sufficient sleep, deepening spirituality, and plenty of good friends tend to support the journey toward wholesome, holistic living.

This book is written as a practical guide for those who would seriously undertake becoming a fine musician. However, since most people who learn to play musical instruments will not become professional musicians, emphasis is placed on enjoying your instrument and learning to perform well so that you and your instrument will be life-long companions. Some will go on to Carnegie Hall while most will play in local symphonies, bands, musical groups, churches, and social gatherings. These are all legitimate reasons to learn to both enjoy and to play music, regardless of how you choose to earn a livelihood. For those who become teachers, lawyers, doctors, and other occupations, there is considerably less time for individual practice. The same lessons apply to all, except that those who will become professional musicians will devote more waking hours to "bonding" with your instrument. In any event, unless you become part of your instrument and it becomes a positive part of you – you will inevitably develop a relationship with your instrument that will only aggravate and insult you, the audience and the instrument!

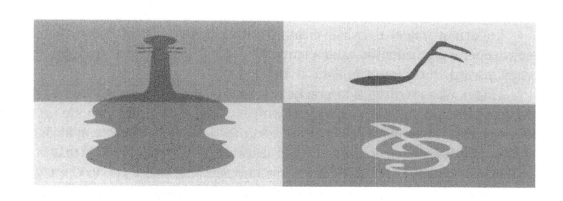

"Opus" (plural: " opuses") – a major work or composition,
"Opuscule" – a minor work – like this book and many of our
performances!

A DOZEN IS GOOD - A BAKER'S DOZEN IS ONE BETTER!

SIX   SEVEN

FIVE   EIGHT

FOUR   NINE

THREE   TEN

TWO   ELEVEN

ONE   TWELVE

13 13 **13 THIRTEEN** 13 13 13

THE LUCKY NUMBER!

2

OPUS ONE

"The world is richer than it is possible to express in any language."
                                                                  –Ilya Prigogine

"Music is capable of expressing our rich world better than any verbal language."
                                                                  –Richard H. Cox

A BAKER'S DOZEN
OF EASY LESSONS WE MUST LEARN

When I was a kid, we went to the local grocery store and bought "windmill" cookies out of the cardboard boxes. They were sold in the "bulk". There were no plastic bags, and cookies were not individually sealed in anything. Plus the fact that if you bought twelve you got thirteen for the same price -- a "baker's dozen". You will find that the thirteenth lesson in this list is like the "free" cookie -- it is given freely without being asked for, and will taste better than the first twelve!

Even if you disagree with the basic assumption of any one of the lessons, don't throw it away. We learn both from those with whom we agree and from those with whom we disagree. These basic lessons make for great discussion groups, personal experiments, and opportunities to measure and determine whether we are simply learning to be a good instrument "technician" or are really becoming a musician.

LESSON ONE

Music Is Essential In Every Person's Life.

There is no one, any where, any place, in any situation, that is not affected by music. We are all touched by music in one way or another every day, and almost every minute of every day. Think of the cacophonous blasting of "hard-rock", the nauseous elevator stuff, the noise that refuses to let you hear your friend at the restaurant, the vibrating boom of gigantic auto speakers at a stop light, the stuff you did not choose to listen to on "telephone hold", or the rich organ music in the cathedral. They all invite, call, demand, or otherwise attack our eardrums. Persons who make music, those who teach music, those who sell music, and those who listen (voluntarily or otherwise) are absolutely essential to our society. And, everyone is a musician in his or her own way, either a voluntary or involuntary performer or listener.

Most of us have not thought very much about how much we *need* music. We think of it in terms of "wanting" to hear a certain kind of music. Have you ever noticed that often even when there is not music around us that we have a tune going over and over in our head or that we start to whistle or hum? Some of us hear a "jingle" on the radio or television and in spite of our efforts just can't get it out of our head. As a matter of fact, the more we try to forget it, the more we remember it. I have even had a tune going over in my head while I was dreaming!

Every aspect of our society utilizes music as an integral part. After all, we could say the "Pledge of Allegiance" at the ballpark and have no music at all, but we don't. We sing one of the most difficult of all American songs to sing, "The Star Spangled Banner". What would a football game be without the band, or the parade without the marching bands? Can you imagine a church service, a wedding, or a funeral without music? Regardless of how inharmonious it may sound, could you have a birthday party without "Happy Birthday" being sung out-of-tune!

4

LESSON TWO

No One Can Escape Being Involved In Music.

Even if you try, you can't do it! You cannot disallow music to come into your life. As long as you have ears, you will hear music. Yes, and those with no hearing tell us that they hear it too! By the time we are old enough to "know what kind of music we like" we have been exposed to the kinds that everyone around us likes. There is little wonder that kids who are raised in homes where classical music is played like classical music and those who grow up with country music like country. Some doctors even believe that infants still in their mother's tummy are moving to the sound of music! If not then, certainly soon thereafter, we hear the mother humming, hoping we will drift off to sleep so that she can do the same thing. Then we hear the music box, the radio, the TV, the stereo, and alas now even the computer, the iPod and the cell phone!

Music is everywhere. There is a word for "everywhere"; it is ubiquitous. Music is ubiquitous. You can literally go nowhere in the world and not hear music. The doctor's office, the restaurant, in elevators, and even when you are on "hold" on the telephone – you can't escape it. Although some music may sound "foreign" to our Western ears, it is clearly recognizable as "music". This is true whether it is composed in a major key, a minor key, or using the Occidental world octave or the pentatonic scale used in the Oriental world.

There is little doubt that our physiology becomes involved with music very early in life and that we develop an affinity for certain sounds, and certain combinations of sounds. We know that children hum and sing before they talk. The first utterances of an infant are musical in nature. When I say, "hear", I mean something very different from what goes in through the eardrum. I speak of the body bonding with sound. The tempo of sound invites certain muscle groups to move, the loudness encourages certain thought patterns, the tone encourages attachment or detachment, the rhythm encourages energy or lethargy, and so on.

Several years ago, while talking to our son on the telephone, he held our

5

two-month old grandson to the telephone and I could hear Jonathon humming melodically. I'm sure he knew that he was singing to his grandpa!

Hearing is a complex process. It is possible for the physical ear to experience sound without the ability to interpret it. In those instances the sound is of no value to us. On the other hand, there are times when we cannot physically "pick up" all the words but very quickly comprehend that the situation calls for immediate action. We obviously "hear" with more than our ears. The average sentence can be adequately understood with many less words than any of us use. The entire meaning of a sentence can be comprehended most of the time if we hear only three words; the subject, the verb and the object. The rest of the sentence we fill in with our own meaning. Furthermore, even when we physically hear all of the words of a sentence, we still "hear" what we want and throw the rest of it away.

Being a person with limited hearing capability, I have made a quite careful study of this subject. Many times you can "hear" what someone is saying by observing facial expressions and body language and you need no words at all. Other times you hear every single word and don't have the slightest idea what the other person is saying. Remember that great song, "your lips tell me no, no, but you are saying yes, yes with your eyes".

Even when the ears are working perfectly, we all hear different things literally and by interpretation. Some people can feel the deep bass vibrations and others don't hear them at all. Some of us don't need to hear them – we can feel them. There are those who like the clashing dissonance of "modern" music, and others detest it and say that it hurts their ears! As a matter of fact, hearing involves and requires thought processes and learning. Much as some of us had to "learn" to like spinach (and some of us never did), we must "learn" to like different sounds (and some of us never will!).

The thought processes of our minds cannot be separated from the physical vibrations around us – and of course – music is basically a series of differing vibrations. Western music is based on the vibrations found in the octave. Medieval music was based on the vibrations of the hexachord, and Greek music is based on the vibrations of the tetrachord. When we speak of "A-440", we are talking about a concert pitch based on 440 vibrations per

6

second. The arrangement of vibrations produce tones in differing relationships to each other, hence, different "tunes". If we used the same vibrations in the same sequence, every song would sound alike. The vibrations around us create music of an extremely wide variety ranging from the train whistle to the fire engine siren, to the automobile horn. George Gershwin's composition, *An American in Paris*, with street sounds, horns and noise, demonstrates how vibrations create different sounds that bring daily life and "composed music" into juxtaposition with each other.

Vibrations that make up music take us back to the earliest experiences with vibrations that we have ever experienced. Our "liking" or preference of one kind of music over another may be in no small way determined by our earliest exposures to differing vibrations, even those we experienced before we were born. A fine pianist friend of mine, to whom this book is dedicated, tells the following story about her daughter who is a concert pianist. Her daughter was learning to play a concerto when she remarked that one part came to her much easier than another part. To her amazement, the part that came easy, although it was a more difficult part of the piece, was the part her mother had incessantly practiced while pregnant with this pianist daughter!

The mind and the body feel and respond very differently when they hear a march from when they hear a waltz. Did you every wonder why they don't play waltzes at basketball games or Sousa marches in restaurants? Madison Avenue and other ingenious "marketers" make millions of dollars off of our musical vulnerability. They know that they can influence what we buy, what we eat, and in no small way control our mood by very carefully selecting the music that we will involuntarily hear. "Mood music" is called that because it is known to influence our moods. Restaurants have learned what kind of music will make you order more food and eat faster. Funeral homes know what kind of background music to play so you will buy a "more memorable" funeral! Musicians must become aware that they are not simply "playing music", they are actually changing the way they and their audience are thinking!

Becoming "involved" in music is an interesting concept. It does not mean only playing an instrument, and it does not only mean enjoying listening to music. "Involvement" is a concept that will become clearer as you go through the lessons in this book. The mind, body, and spirit are all involved. We don't even have to be willing to be involved. Involvement doesn't mean "liking" or "not liking" the music. We hear people say, "I just can't get into that kind of music". They are already "into it" or they would not know they do not like it. When the music pushes you to an opinion, when it causes you to make bodily movements, when it forces you to increase or decrease the volume – you are involved. It can really be frustrating when I "don't like the music" so I turn it off, but can't keep from hearing it in my head! That's involvement!

LESSON THREE

Music Is Capable of Soothing Troubled Emotions.

From the beginning of time we have known the therapeutic value of music. It has been said, "music soothes the savage beast". Hymns, many of the classics, folk tunes, spirituals, and many other kinds of music have endured not only because of their musical quality, but also because of their enduring therapeutic value. The earliest African-American slave found solace in "Swing Low Sweet Chariot", and other spirituals that we have had the good fortune of inheriting. Likewise, we have no idea how many troubled souls have found peace in "O God our help through ages past, our hope for years to come".

It has been found that certain kinds of music bring tranquility. You may even have heard some it in your dentist's office. The roving cowboy strummed soothing music on his guitar, the harpist in David's Old Testament days created many soothing psalms, and even the "hobo" whistled away the day. The harp, the guitar, the harmonica, and other instruments were more than musical instruments to their owners, they were companions.

It is interesting that in troubled times as well as in times of celebration people turn to music. Some time ago, I heard a college choir and orchestra perform a marvelous arrangement of "The Battle Hymn of the Republic". Although done well, it was a small college music department. But that did not matter. It had the trumpets, the drums, and most of all the deep feeling, sung by those young voices. The music was stirring and inspiring. It served, as it always does, to identify the audience with the troubled times of our country, and allowed us all to transcend our puny daily "troubles" in the light of tumultuous war-torn days of the past and present. When the speaker, General Norman Schwarzkopf gave his speech it was as if the music started his speech, and that his speech simply continued the music. The mood was set and continued. The music did it.

LESSON FOUR

Music is Capable of Troubling Tranquil Emotions.

Just as music can soothe the troubled soul, it can also trouble the quiet soul. Riots, stampedes, crowds going wild, stadiums in distress, police called in to corral crowds, political revolts, and nationalistic songs, all illustrate some of the newspaper reports we have all read, and demonstrate the sometimes troublesome power of music. A parade without music would be like lightning without thunder. A human-rights demonstration without "We Shall Overcome" would simply not be the same. The rhythmic chants at a ballgame, and the cries of the crowd at a horserace are all musical sounds of heightened emotions. Many musical compositions and performances are often intended to trouble the soul and provoke emotions to bring about changes in our thinking.

Music changes emotions and can evoke aggression, even rage. It is said that at one point in history the bagpipe was declared a weapon of war because it had the ability to so enrage the emotions. We have the illustration in the Old Testament of Joshua fighting the battle of Jericho. He used blaring trumpets as he surrounded the city. According to the Bible, it worked. Never doubt what can happen when you blow a horn!

Music in our time has been a primary catalyst in consciousness raising. The "boom-box" of a former year was only the forerunner of the gigantic sub-woofers in today's cars. They all tended to play music that could be characterized as aggressive. "Hard-rock", "heavy metal", and "rap" are negatively stimulating and many believe lead to aggressive behavior. I don't think I have ever heard Brahms or Handel from boom-boxes or automobile sub-woofers!

By the same token, there were Christian hymns that were intended to lead to aggressive action. "Onward Christian Soldiers" is certainly in that category. Music can incite revolt just as it will incite retreat. The important message is that music can and does produce an energy that leads to action.

10

LESSON FIVE

Music Changes Both the Performer and the Listener.

It has been said that "no man steps into the same stream twice". We could also say that no one performs or listens to the same music twice. The emotions and the actual technique of playing is never the same even when performing the same piece on the same instrument. How often we have all found that a rehearsal can "go well", and the performance is less than desired. We have also experienced the simply terrible rehearsal, yet the performance went well. There are hundreds of reasons for this. Everything from what we ate for lunch to the reaction of the audience. The astute listener can add hundreds of reasons why what is heard is not the same each time.

We need only to observe the bored person trying to stay awake (and sometimes not succeeding), sitting right beside another person who is animated, even moving to the rhythm of the music, to understand the effect that the same performer and the same music can have on two different persons. Recently I was attending a symphony concert and observed this actual scene. The interesting thing was that on a subsequent piece of music, the gentleman who was asleep started moving his head with the music and his female companion went to sleep!

The deeper lesson, however, is that what we hear becomes indelibly written in our minds. We will talk later about memory. But suffice it to say here that sound waves are physical and the changes that occur in our brains that allow us to "hear" are electrical, chemical, and physical, and as a result they are not just "sounds", they are brain changes! No wonder that music has the ability to change us as persons. This may explain why music played to infants still in the womb effects the baby in demonstrative and measurable ways. Language development, personality development, and much more that we do not as yet know, are the result of what the baby hears *before* it is born! There is certainly every physiological and psychological reason that such should be the fact. Remember, when you perform, plan for it to change you and everyone that hears you, even those in the womb – because it will!

LESSON SIX

Music Teaches Independence, Dependence, and Interdependence.

There is probably no better teaching tool than music to demonstrate the value of learning to participate in integrative, harmonious, teamwork. It teaches absolute *independence* upon one's own abilities and self-confidence. Likewise, it teaches that without *dependence* upon other performers and the conductor, music can become terrible noise. It also shares with many sports the fact that unless there is *interdependence*, i.e., teamwork, that there could be many wonderful "plays" but no common goal. We have all heard instrumental and vocal groups that seemed to be made up of many soloists rather than a harmonious group.

When we hear a duet or quartet in which each of the performers is aware of every nuance of the other performers, it sounds like a solo but made up of several parts. It is easy to detect the difference when performers do not keep an eye on the conductor. "Followership" is essential to good music-making. Yet, in music, like in many participatory activities, good followers are also good leaders, but choose to lead their own performance by following someone else! Those who choose to do otherwise will invariably come in late or start ahead of the conductor. This is the critical balance between dependence and independence, and the result of interdependence.

LESSON SEVEN

The Least Important Reason to Learn To Play an Instrument is to be Able to Perform.

Every music teacher knows that apart from the spring recital, the band concert, or the operetta, that most children who "take music lessons" will not in fact perform much beyond that point in their lives. In fact, the vast majority of music students will never develop the skills adequate for future public performance. Most children typically take lessons for a year or two, sing a couple of years in junior high or high school, but soon give up the attempt to really learn how to play or sing.

That is not the question – and it may not even be important. We ask, "to what end is the benefit of all this work", and "why do we spend so much money in taking lessons", if the student will never become a good musician? There are many important benefits. Far too many to discuss here, however, suffice it to say that music is a language. It speaks to the soul. Life-long, long-lasting, fulfillment factors come into play. The same thing is true of music that is true of ballet, skating, or other performance arts. Children learn self-confidence, poise, teamwork, social skills, the knowledge of timing, and much more. The good music teacher teaches much more than music. The best ones are therapists of the finest sort.

We have all heard that we study music to become "cultured". That may be true, but more importantly, we study music to become ourselves. We "find" ourselves in music. The coordination of body-parts requires a rhythm of the person, the listening skills attune us to the sounds of life, the performance skills transfer to whatever we do as a profession, and the discipline is universal to everything that we will ever do.

LESSON EIGHT

The Musical Skills we Learn are Important to Personality Growth.

Personality development is not well understood. Certainly genetic as well as environmental factors play huge, maybe even equal roles. Personality is much more than the accumulation of skills, however, we have all observed what the effect of being clumsy does to a child's personality. Likewise, we have observed what the effect of being well-disciplined does to a child. Children, like all of us who are adults, *do what they are*. But they also *are what they do*. Doing has a profound effect upon becoming. Skills that give poise and self-confidence promote healthy personality growth.

If we observe the tiny infant we find that only large muscle control is possible. The child grasps with the whole hand. As the infant develops, there is increased fine motor control and it can pick things up with the thumb and index finger, known as prehensile grasp, a form of physical function unique to the human being. At first the child sees only something moving, then later recognizes that the "thing" has parts and that the mobile above the crib is made up of many pieces. These are all parts of both physical and personality development. The ability to translate a sensation from the finger to the brain, then to tell the brain to do something that the finger wants to do is an unbelievable neurological process. We can see the physiological activity easily. We can see the personality activity easily too if we observe how fast the child activates the finger, how tentatively or aggressively the child moves, and how shy or outgoing the child behaves.

Personality and physical behavior go hand in hand. The extrovert tends to be outgoing in all ways. The introvert tends to be retiring and quiet in all ways. The physical actions of these two types of personalities are not always consistent with the type, however, for the most part, they are. As a result, a different type of personality may do better in playing Wagner than Liszt. Concert musicians will attest that it takes a conscious mind-set to switch from one mood of music to another. They often must consciously make a change in their style of thinking, therefore their physical action, in order to play the piece with the composer's feeling. Keeping the mind and body together is not automatic. The personality will win every time unless the brain takes control of both the body and the emotions.

Music allows us to teach many lessons of real living without saying a word. It allows these lessons to be learned from within. Internally learned lessons are more lasting and better integrated into the whole of one's personality than lessons that are "preached". Music lessons are personality-building sessions.

LESSON NINE

Music Requires Every Intellectual Skill and Engages Every Academic Subject.

The best way to illustrate this point is to discuss it in the light of a standard intelligence test, specifically the Wechsler Intelligence Scale which is the most popular of the many "I.Q" tests. This test is divided into three categories. The first is the "verbal" portion which requires recall of specific bits of information from a pool of general knowledge. Some of the bits of information come from history, geography, literature, and other commonly learned academic areas of study. The "performance" portion of the test includes things like arranging blocks into patterns, deciphering codes, and recognizing patterns of process and sequence. When these two portions are "scored", they are numerically compared to the scores of other persons who are the same age, and a "full scale", i.e., total score is derived.

As one inspects this standard "I.Q." test carefully it is easily seen that music includes every subject and the entire gamut of both "verbal" and "performance" skills. Most of human learning is basically memory. We remember how to repeat a verbal or motor skill that produces a given specific end result. There is no better manual or mental exercise for learning the application of memory to motor skills than learning how to play a musical instrument. The tiresome, yet essential, memorization and tedious practice of "running scales", "playing the chromatics", and other "boring" exercises lay a foundation for both understanding and utilizing the knowledge we obtain and use in virtually every educational pursuit.

In music we have notation, timing, tones, volume, sequence, adding, subtracting, utilization of symbols, and even understanding bits of foreign language. The learning of musical skills takes us back into history and forward into mathematics. It requires knowledge of literature and the ability to understand other cultures. We must help children to understand that every subject they study will help them in becoming a fine musician, and that every thing they learn in music will help them in becoming a fine doctor, lawyer, mother, father, or anything else they will ever become.

LESSON TEN

Music Builds Mental, Physical, Social, and Spiritual Awareness.

Discipline is the key word for virtually all that we learn as human beings. There is no better method for "disciplining" the mind and body than that required in order to become a musician. Some people see discipline as "punishment" for wrong-doing. Not so. Discipline is the art of making a disciple. A disciple is a follower who hopefully becomes an example like his/her leader. We must discipline, i.e. train by repeated thinking and action, the mind, the body, and the emotions to produce a desired end result. This is true in many athletic pursuits as well. Whether it be in playing a chromatic scale on the keyboard, playing "long tones" on a wind instrument, learning to produce a smooth "drum roll", or integrating the eyes, ears, hands, and feet on a pipe organ, the discipline is the same.

In order to build a proper discipline base, one must attempt to understand the times in which a given composer produced the work, the instrument upon which is was first played, the political, social, religious, and economic circumstances of the era, and much more. The physical dexterity, the mental alertness, the reason for producing the music, and the potential governmental intrusion

16

even have to be considered. We sometimes forget that music, like literature, was often seen as a political statement. More than one composer paid a political price to publish and perform a musical work.

The spiritual nature of learning music cannot be overstated. Much of the great classical music we enjoy today is the result of weekly command performances in the great cathedrals of Europe. Certainly one has only to think of Bach's organ compositions to recognize the truth of this point.

LESSON ELEVEN

Music Includes and Transcends All Races, Creeds, Colors, Sexes, and Nations.

This lesson seems so self-evident that it should not need to be mentioned. Music has always been recognized as "the universal language". The earliest generations of the human race certainly considered music extremely important. Biblical literature records that Adam's grandson Jubal played the harp and the lute. Even though a specific form of music may have arisen from a given ethnic groups or for religious purposes, we know that music is rarely limited to a specific audience. Most everyone listens to virtually every kind of music – even the kinds they don't like! A good musician draws upon many kinds of music regardless of whether the emphasis is upon classical, contemporary, or soul music. Everyone seems to have some inner part that identifies with most any kind of music that is heard. It is interesting to hear a person say that they "hate country music", but then to watch as they unconsciously start to tap their foot to the beat of the music they "hate". Or to hear a person say, "I wouldn't listen to a note of opera", only to have them ask, "why are they singing in a foreign language?" When we encounter a different beat, a different sequence of chords, and different styles of expression, we are forced to experience the cultures of the world.

There are distinctive styles of musical composition and expression that arise out of different styles of living. It is interesting to hear the music of a culture whose artwork is primarily composed of square and straight lines, as opposed to the music which comes out of a culture where the artwork is flowing, spiral, and swirling. Each culture produces a music that speaks to its collective connection with earth, life, soul, and after-life.

My professional consultation work has taken me into many foreign countries. I have noticed that the style of life, the dress, the social customs, the religion, and much more can be vividly seen in the musical expressions of the country. The political times can be detected in much music, even those of the classical composers of Europe. One has only to observe our own musical expressions to see the same thing. The military march speaks to the formality and orderly structure of the army. The waltz demonstrates the free flowing movement of a Strauss era in Europe. Each of these styles, and all other styles, demonstrate distinctly different cultures and ways of thinking.

The best illustration of the cross-cultural nature of music is the opera. Just think of the vocalist singing in harmony with the orchestra, using words from a "foreign" language, and dressed in a costume associated with a different time and place. We immediately see culture, spirituality, politics, literature, history, art, religion, family values, national interests, and far more ethnic, religious, and gender issues than can be discussed here.

LESSON TWELVE

The Least Valuable Result of Studying Music is Learning to Play an Instrument.

After discussing the broad and inclusive values of learning to play an instrument or to sing, it seems ridiculous to make this statement, however it is true. So often we get caught up in the "correct fingering", the "correct embouchure", and other technicalities. These items are important, even imperative. But that is not the point of this lesson. We have already discussed that only a few of the many students will eventually end up performing professionally. Skill, technique, and ability are still important, even if we play for our own amusement. The point at hand, however, is that technique and method are of no value in and of themselves. They are only of value when coupled with the overall picture of accomplishment, personality development, spiritual integration, and produced by an emotionally strong person.

Learning music is just another way of learning to live life. The instrument, or the voice, is simply an avenue – which is exactly what we call it – an instrument. The instrument becomes an extension of our innermost person and simply conveys our inner voice in a different way. We cannot forget that the "whole is greater than the sum of the parts". The parts that we learn are lessons in memory, skill building, visual and auditory learning, self-confidence, social awareness, and on and on. The whole of this learning is the integration of each of us into a meaningful, deeply spiritual life that is built upon memory and discipline. Virtually everything we will ever do, regardless of our chosen life style or profession will be the result of memory and discipline.

LESSON THIRTEEN

The Most Valuable Contribution of Music is the Dynamic Force Conveyed Through –YOUR Personality!

Have you ever wondered how a given teacher captivates even the most disinterested student and other teachers cannot challenge even the most interested pupil? Or, why teachers who teach "identically" the same lesson with the "same teaching method" end up with such very different results? The answer to these questions is usually, "the student just isn't interested", or some other displaced excuse onto the student, or "there is no encouragement at home". Although both of these statements may be true in various cases, they are, nonetheless, rationalizations and excuses, not answers.

This is the thirteenth of the "baker's dozen". The number thirteen is considered by many to be an unlucky number. Not so in this case – even on Friday the 13th! This is the bonus lesson. To learn this lesson is to culminate all of the others into a valuable gem that will under-gird all of life. A teacher and a student are a team. Blame and credit must be shared. Maybe not equally to be sure, but more often than not, even though when we are teachers we would rather not look at our part. We have already recognized that sometimes the most important part of learning music is not the learning how to play an instrument or to sing. It is how to live life. The personality of the teacher and pupil are magnified through the instrument or the voice.

We all know it is difficult to teach someone who does not wish to be taught. However, again, our job is to teach life using the trumpet, piano, or violin as the "instrument" to do so. Our task *includes* teaching, but is *much more* than teaching. It is expressing our personality in a way that is contagious. The student will attempt to play like the teacher. This requires thinking like the teacher. Teachers become idolized or disliked. They are examples and role models of what the student would like to be, or not like to be. The experienced music critic can often identify with whom a performer has studied by observing their style and technique. This fact should be sobering to every music teacher!

20

Whether you are the student or the teacher, the expression of yourself as "a person" is the most valuable end result of music. Music is an avenue. It is a pathway. It is a road. It is another journey in life whereby we learn who we are and how we influence ourselves and others, hopefully for better, whether we intend to do so or not.

OPUS TWO

"It isn't what we don't know that makes us ignorant, it's what we know that isn't so."
—F.T. H'Doubler, Sr., M.D.

"Believing that which is not so prohibits us from discovering the truth."
—Richard H. Cox

SYMBOLS AND RITUALS IN MUSIC

Symbols and rituals are the things living is made of. ***Everything we do is some kind of a combination of symbols and rituals.*** There is probably no other activity in the world in which this statement is more true than it is in music.

Symbols are individual "things" that come to have a specific meaning. For instance, the wedding band is clearly a symbol of "being married". The traffic stop sign at the corner has a specific meaning. However, neither of these "things" is a ritual. A ritual is the combination of many symbols. For instance, a bride, a groom, wedding rings, and a ceremony combine together to make a ritual.

One could think of each note of music as a symbol. But individual notes do not make music. Music is made only when many notes are combined to make a tune. The individual notes have meaning but do not tell a whole story. The whole composition including hundreds and thousands of notes, when put together form a ritual that tells a story. This is even more understandable when we put several pieces together to form an opera, an oratorio, or a musical play. The individual notes do not tell you about that wonderful, bewildered father in *Fiddler On The Roof.* However, when all the notes are put together in many small songs, the story comes together and a ritual is developed with which we can identify.

Identification is the key. If we had never seen a stop sign, we would not know what it means or what to do. If we had never seen a wedding band, we would just think it is another ring on the finger. This is illustrated by persons who are unaware that a European custom is often to wear the wedding band on the right rather than the left hand. Americans sometimes do not recognize the ring as a wedding band because they see it as being on the "wrong hand". The symbol must be in the understood place to have meaning. An experiment was done several years ago by reversing the order of the red, yellow and green traffic lights. The red light was put on the bottom and the green light on the top. Motorists were incredibly confused and some even went on red and stopped on green! That is because meaning is taught.

Our hearing is conditioned by the symbols of "our kind" of music. Western music gets its meaning from "our own scale". We are used to the octave scale of musical composition, therefore it sounds familiar. Most of our music is composed using the diatonic scale. When we hear music composed on other scales, such as the pentatonic scale, it sounds strange. You can hear some people say that some music sounds "foreign". Some of our "modern" music sounds dissonant and "wrong" because we are not used to the succession of symbols (notes) that make up that particular ritual (composition).

When we play music it must communicate meaning to those who hear it. The notes must follow a pattern we understand, and the succession of notes must all go together to produce a whole piece that we can "register" in our minds. We may not "like" the whole piece (the ritual), but then, there are rituals we do not "like". On the other hand, our inner person may "harmonize" with it easily. This usually means that we have had a previous inner experience that understands that particular ritual (arrangement) of notes. An easy way to understand this is to play a series of chords and leave the seventh tone hanging. Everyone awaits the resolution to the tonic chord. This doesn't mean that resolution to the tonic chord is "right" or "wrong", but for most people it "sounds right". Our symbolic interpretation of a ritual of notes requires a recognizable resolution in order to make the ritual mean what we think it is supposed to mean. If you want to experiment with this, play the little ditty, "Shave and a haircut, two-bits", and leave off the last note, or "Happy Birthday" and leave off the last note. Inevitably, we have to put that last note on, at least in our minds, and usually in sound!

Symbols and rituals in music provide all kinds of benefits for us. For instance, they bridge years. You can be taken back to childhood by hearing "Ring Around the Rosy", "Jesus Loves Me", or some other song that had meaning for you as a child. This music allows you to "connect" with your past and with the things in your life that had meaning at that time in your life. Connecting with our past experiences, and with the feelings of other cultures and times are doubtless some of the most valuable aspects of the ritual of music.

Symbols and rituals allow us to gain insight and understanding of ourselves and others. When we really listen to music from a different culture than our own, we can hear the joy, the grief, the pathos, or the purpose of that music. For instance, African drums bring to us an all together different understanding than that of the snare drum in an approaching parade. The blare of the trumpet in the bull-ring gives us a different understanding than the trumpet paying *Taps* at a military funeral. Then, too, they both give us a totally different understanding than when we hear the trumpet in *"The Trumpet Shall Sound"* from *The Messiah.*

The symbols and rituals of music provide meaning to myth. For instance, we know that *Peter and the Wolf* is a myth. Yet when all of the instruments play the many notes of that ritual, we are able to put together a very personal meaning to a story that now is "real", but in truth is still only a myth.

Symbols and rituals, particularly the symbols of music, are capable of emotional healing. Ask almost anyone about a song that made them laugh, made them cry, made them happy or made them sad, and they will tell you that this is so. Why is this? It is because our emotions are constantly seeking wholeness. Our emotions look for opportunities to put life together in a meaningful way. Music, particularly, songs or pieces that have been with us in "special times", frequently allows this to happen. Just think about our choice of music for important occasions. Why do we choose certain musical pieces for weddings, funerals or celebrations? It is because those songs have a special meaning to us and bring the past into focus with the present. Think of the songs that are chosen for funerals. They frequently are ones that the deceased person loved. By playing or singing them, we can identify with our past, the deceased person's past, and focus on putting the present together with the future. The same is true with songs chosen for weddings and other special occasions.

How is it that symbols and rituals actually work? This is not hard to understand. Symbols use those bits of communication that we already understand and accept. They allow us to put a value on things without putting it into words. They are understood in a fashion that does not allow argument. Even though others might vigorously differ on the meaning of a particular symbol, our own meaning is so deeply imbedded in us that we are not easily shaken. The meaning comes from the "inner" person so that even if we don't like the sound or the whole piece of music, the symbols and rituals are authentic and we can't question their purpose. They are deep in feeling as over against intellectual. They transcend both time and space. They can transport us to magical places and to magical thinking.

This is why it is so important that you choose the correct piece to play for a specific occasion. The succession of notes bring out joy, sorrow, and all sorts of emotions and most importantly tie the audience, individually, back to other points of meaning and other times in their lives.

Understanding how our music allows all of us to connect with our past, get beyond our present, and permit us to be transported to a magical future is just the tip of the iceberg in the appreciation of symbols and rituals in music.

OPUS THREE

TRANSCENDENCE – THE POWER OF PERFORMANCE

In order to fully understand and appreciate the message of this opus, it is necessary to first understand two words. They are *"transcendence"*, and *"imminence"*. The word "transcendence" means to produce something far greater, higher, and more lofty than the foundation it represents. It means to go beyond. The word "imminence" connotes that something dreadful is about to happen. Imminence is devoid of creativity, hope, and reason for anything but survival needs. Transcendence allows for creativity, growth, hope, and a reason to let survival needs take care of themselves, while you get on with being a great musician. When you talk about "stage fright", you are talking about "imminence". You are paralyzed by what you think is something dreadful that

29

is about to happen. When you get rid of that neurotic thinking, you are free to soar with the eagles and not worry about all the dangers down below. That's transcendence!

What is it that we transcend? We transcend the piece of wood or brass we call an instrument. We transcend our training and even our experience. We transcend the audience in front of us. Frequently we must transcend a headache, a cold, or other physical ailments. We must transcend our negative thoughts and fears. And, most of all, we transcend ourselves.

We transcend the instrument we are playing. The instrument becomes an extension of ourselves and when we are properly "bonded" to it, it becomes just another part of our person. It speaks for us. It communicates for us. Any instrument is by itself wood, brass, or material of some sort. St. Paul reminded us that without love we become 'tinkling brass', which indicates the emptiness of material without transcendence.

We also transcend the music. Music is notes. Black marks on paper. Even when played, notes are just noise unless controlled. Music can sound empty even when it is played technically correct. It has a "hollow-ring" to it unless it communicates a message with feeling. Transcendence allows us to lift the music to a height of spiritual quality which is discernible by the audience. It is also observable to the performer. When performing, the performer can see the transcendence in the audience and the audience can see it in the performer. You may not be able to define it, or to identify exactly what you are experiencing, but you know it is there.

We transcend the performance itself. Some concerts are a series of musical pieces. They may sound wonderful and everyone comments on how technically well they were performed, or even how great it sounded. But in other concerts that actually may not be as well executed there is "something else" happening. People are brought to tears, or to laughter, or taken back to childhood, or transported to another place and other time. This is transcendence. It raises the performance to a place that is easily felt but indefinable.

Those who remain in the imminent (day to day stuff) suffer from performance anxiety and fear. While they talk about self-confidence, they actually are planning for the dread of the next moment. They have not found solace in knowing how to conquer imminence, thereby allowing them to create, hope, and transcend themselves, their instrument, the music, and even the audience!

Stage fright is not fright of the stage. It is fright of oneself. When we transcend, or get beyond ourselves, there is no fear of ourselves. Getting outside your own body and mind is not easy, yet it can be done. The great artists of all time, whether in music, or in other artistic fields, have surmounted themselves with a vision, a dream, aspirations, and raptures that have taken them outside their physical bodies into a spiritual realm. This spiritual, transcendent, realm allowed them to forget fear. None of the great painters worried that people would not like their art. And, in many instances the public of their generation did not like it. Only many years after they were dead did their work become appreciated – and for that matter- bring any money! Many great musicians were ignored, ridiculed, and even persecuted by the public and government officials. Leonard Bernstein, for instance, was officially blacklisted in America's McCarthy era. Many Jewish composers in Germany were persecuted by the Nazis. Wagner's politics were always getting him into trouble. Judge Vladimir Stiborik of Czechoslovakia sentenced some jazz musicians to jail as recently as 1987. Yet, these musicians and many others show us how their spiritual inspiration drove them to higher levels of transcendence and musical accomplishments.

The imminent (everyday things) ties you to your own failure. Every "wrong" note that you have ever played comes to mind and the judgement of every parental figure comes out of the woodwork. Performance anxiety is just that, anxiety. Anxiety is caused by not knowing what is going to happen and the fear of not being able to control it.

The opposite of anxiety is excitement. Anxious feelings can be turned into creative energy. The performer who is always excited about the music, the instrument, the audience, and most importantly the message about to be played, will not have disabling anxiety. He or she will have a creative excitement about "finalizing" in front of an audience what has been tediously practiced in the private studio.

To be imminent is to be earth bound. This means that you are literally tied to the stage, to your skin, to your trembling, to your mistakes, to your

31

critics, and to your failure! Being tied to that kind of stuff is baggage that will destroy the best of performers. Great performers are frequently criticized for being egotistical, arrogant, and aloof. While these are certainly not necessary attributes to be a great musician, it is understandable that some develop these characteristics to "climb over" the obstacles of being imminent, or tied to the things that would hinder their transcendence.

It is a real art to be able to transcend the imminent without becoming obnoxious. But it can be done. How is this accomplished? It requires a special kind of thinking. One kind for personal and interpersonal relationships, and another for the "stage personality". One can be humble with others and relate to people as a "real human", yet when approaching the stage, it is possible and necessary to surround oneself with a confidence that insulates you from everything except your performance. This is not arrogance. It is competent performance technique.

When we stand up to speak, we know (or at least we *should* know), what we are going to say. Hopefully our talk is more than mere words. Words are like your instrument. Our voice and its words are simply the mechanism for getting the message out. We have a message we want to give. We have a statement we want to make. We have a point to make. The musician-performer who has properly prepared for the performance will do the same. The instrument is only the megaphone for the point we want to make and the message we want to give. The speaker will stumble over a word or two, maybe breathe at the wrong place, or even have to cough, or believe it or not have to belch! But the question is not whether any of these things happened. The question is whether the audience heard the message and got the point!

There are numerous instances of composers who literally transcended themselves. Probably one of the most illustrative is Handel who essentially went into a sequestered fugue state for 24 days while he continuously wrote the *Messiah*. He was lifted to a height of inspiration that we still feel to this day. No one can hear the "Hallelujah Chorus" without experiencing his transcendent experience. Transcendence takes the performer out of the imminent (day to day earthbound) and into a loftier, higher, spiritual place. It is the state of true inspiration. The state we always seek but rarely experience. On the occasions when we have had just a small hint of transcendence, we are electrified by the inspiration and know it deeply inside. In transcendent performance the performer is eclipsed by the music; the music is eclipsed by the experience; and the experience is eclipsed by the changes that take place in the spiritual center of both the listener and the performer!

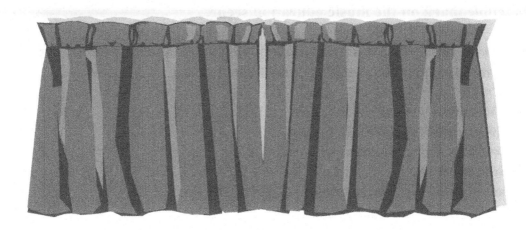

by
Michael A. Davison, DMA

Whether I am teaching at the Interlochen Arts Camp or at the University of Richmond, I've become aware of two governing elements: 1) the ever-changing, fast-paced world and 2) The climate in which we teach. The students of today have to learn reams of information, develop many performance techniques, at a much greater speed and alacrity. Due to this pace, the young musicians acquire handicaps – physical, emotional and psychological blocks. As a performer, I try to channel my energies and direct my teaching to help the young artist, all the while blending my teaching to include the areas aforementioned. I've had the opportunity to study Dr. Cox as a private teacher, performer, and lecturer, working with many young musicians. Dr. Cox encapsulates the finest teaching in this area – he can speak to these different areas and get to the crux of the physical and psychological blocks quickly. Through Dr. Cox's guidance, they obtain almost instantaneous results. Richard Cox has crafted his ideas and pedagogy into a study guide for the young performer. I use his refreshing concepts in my studio and in my daily performance life. Dr. Cox has made an indelible mark on the music education scene.

Thank you Richard for not only bringing your gifts to the printed page, but sharing these principles with my students and me.

Dr. Michael Davison
Professor of Trumpet/Jazz
University of Richmond
Richmond, VA
Director of Brass, Interlochen Center for the Arts

OPUS FOUR

"To my mind there must be, at the bottom of it all, not an equation, but an utterly simple idea. And to me that idea, when we finally discover it, will be so compelling, so inevitable, that we will say to one another, 'Oh, how beautiful. How could it have been otherwise?"
     –John Archibald Wheeler

"Every composition is a series of phrases, and every phrase a series of notes, and every note a solo."

–Richard H. Cox

THE BRAIN, BODY, AND MUSICAL PERFORMANCE

The body and brain are functionally inseparable, however, it is helpful to consider them as individual parts of our anatomy for purposes of understanding how they work. The combination of the brain and the body may be viewed as a large corporation housed in a huge office complex. The brain is the master control-room of the entire building and the organizational management for all of the corporation's business, filing systems, bookkeeping duties, planning, marketing, sales, and delivery systems. The body, for the most part, provides the equipment for all of those functions. Until the brain says, "deliver", the store-room cannot pull anything out of its inventory. Until the brain says, "enter", the bookkeeping system cannot enter the price of an object or invoice for a sale.

So it is with musical performance. The brain provides the decision-making apparatus that tells the body to move the fingers, the feet, the lips, or whatever part of the body is required for playing a given instrument. It also tells the vocal cords, throat, tongue, mouth, and breathing parts what to do for singing a given note. The mind and the body act in concert whether the performer wishes them to do so or not. When the lips of the trumpet player are spaced to play a certain note, the mind has already given the command to do so, even if it is the "wrong" note. The physical movement produced is always the "right" note according to the brain's command. The only exception to this is when there is neurological dysfunction resulting from various brain defects.

There is much written regarding the "left" brain and the "right" brain. It is helpful to understand some of this highly complex information. The brain is divided into two major parts within our skulls. These sections are called "hemispheres; the "left" hemisphere, and the "right" hemisphere. There is a master "switchboard" called the thalamus that separates out signals and channels them to the appropriate part of the brain. This somewhat egg-shaped mass of gray matter is positioned deeply within the brain and literally integrates all of our sensory information that comes from joints, ears, eyes, skin, and everywhere on and in our body. It also is responsible for handling the input that keeps our mind alert. Furthermore, it works with another part of the brain called the hypothalamus that deals with emotional responses to incoming stimuli. The thalamus then sends these messages on to the cortex. The cortex, particularly the part behind our forehead (called the frontal cortex) is the part that lets us make decisions that are reasonable, organized, and socially appropriate. Another important part of the brain is the mygdale. There is an mygdale (like other sections of the brain) on each side of the brain – inside and not far from the ears. This part of the brain interprets stimuli and gives negative (even angry) or positive energy to actions. These and other parts of our brain make up what we call the "executive" function of our behavior. It's kind of like what happens in an executive office; i.e., making decisions, scheduling appointments, being polite and appropriate, and causing everything to work in harmony. The thalamus is like an complex electrical switchboard. Sort of like a musical mixer board that channels and manages sound. It serves both sides of the brain.

In music it is necessary to use both parts of the brain. One part keeps time, for instance, and the other part puts in the feeling. There is another part of the brain that we don't understand as completely as we would like. It is called the corpus callosum. This part connects both sides of the brain together with a very complicated network. It may turn out to be one of the most important parts of the brain's ability to integrate complex activity and to allow both sides of the brain to work at the same time. The "left" side of the brain is believed to be the more analytical and rational. The "right" side of the brain is believed to be the more artistic, creative, and emotional. However, we are far from understanding either side of the brain, and more importantly, how they work together.

Understanding the brain is for the musician kind of like it is for the driver to understand the automobile's mechanics. You don't have to know anything about valves, carburetors, valves, fuel pump, and so on in order to drive a car well. However, this knowledge provides a depth of understanding you are glad to have, particularly when things go wrong. The same is true of the brain. A good musician does not need to know how the brain works. It is helpful, however, to understand that the brain is a very complex mechanism and that various kinds of practice influence and train different parts of the brain for professional performance. Students who have difficulty "being interested" in finger exercises on the piano keyboard are not necessarily disinterested, but instead, they may actually lack the motor coordination that makes playing those exercises less difficult.

If things are harder, for whatever reason, we are often not interested in those activities. We find that persons who are unfeeling in general are also unfeeling in music. However, ***the brain can be trained.*** The parts of music (and other things in life) that come harder for us and require more practice may be due to differing neurological abilities in our individual brains. Sometimes it helps to realize that the brain *can* be trained. We have even discovered that new brain cells are born for as long as we live, and that there is no age limit on "new learning". The brain learns very much like computer systems – repetition, programming, more repetition and more programming. Some folks seem to think of the brain as something that "thinks" but doesn't really "do things". ***The brain is very much a working mechanism and as such requires practice just as other parts of our body that we are trying to strengthen.***

It is also important to understand the complexity of the brain to fully appreciate all that goes into what we call memory. The stuff that memory is made of is incredibly complex and still not very well understood. It may be that each brief chemical and electrical message that is passed from one nerve cell to another changes the chemical and electrical acceptance or rejection at the next nerve junction. These junctions are called "synapses". They are not unlike the contacts in an electronic organ or a computer. We do know one thing for certain, and that is, in order for the brain to "remember", it requires repeated electrochemical experiences of the same sort. With repeated experiences the impression becomes at least a temporary imprint on the brain. Repetition no doubt strengthens this process and becomes what we call memory. Although this is a very simple and less than scientifically accurate description of the brain's function in memory, it serves to help us to understand the necessity of constant practice to keep those synapses firing.

Everything we do in life is the result of memory. The moment we are born we begin to remember – and to forget! We remember things and then forget parts of what we remembered. Each time we repeat that learning experience we remember a bit more and forget a bit less. Eventually, a given bit of knowledge is imbedded (literally stamped) in a relatively permanent fashion – but only as long as we continue to reinforce it. There was a famous psychologist by the name of Piaget who called the process of memory "engramming". I have always liked that characterization because it is in truth something like putting a brand on cattle. Its not just a thought, the memory really gets stamped (programmed) into the brain. The memory literally gets embedded on the limbic system (the memory part), and imprinted. Although I know that it takes repetition and constant reinforcement to keep the memory there, it gives me a sense of making things that I remember at least semi-permanent. Just think of all you must remember to play an instrument! Then think of the tremendous amount of information elderly persons have acquired – no wonder they forget things!

Professionals talk about two basic kinds of memory; long term and short term. In actuality, memory is a continuum from immediate memory through intermediate, to long term, then on to very long term. When you stop to think about it, if we live to become seventy years old, there is an incredible amount of information to be remembered. By the time we are only a few months old we have learned and remembered how to perform many of the basic elements of human behavior. When we begin to train our memory to perform music, we call upon many of the early memories from our infancy. All the way through life we continue to call upon the memories of earlier times to perform the activities of the day and to acquire new memories.

Frequently "stage fright" is not a fear of the moment, but the uncomfortable recollection of earlier experiences that get translated in the now. Memory is far more than a "mental thing". Memory brings back the shakes, the sweating, the anxious breathing, and all of the other physiological and mental anguishes that we do not want. In other words, when the brain functions, it does so as a whole. We can't just remember things in our head. When we remember things, we remember them in our whole body.

It seems that when the brain is functioning normally that it tends to do so as a single unit. However, when a single part of the brain malfunctions there are interesting and strange things that happen. This is because language is in one part of the brain, art is in another, and so on. When one part malfunctions it does not necessarily alter the way other parts function, although there are usually repercussions throughout the brain, sometimes in subtle and other times in major ways.

We have evidence from the lives of actual persons that language is located on one side of the brain and music on the other, however, there is also evidence that the two sides communicate. The communication may be the function of the thalamus we talked about, or the corpus callosum that serves as a connecting link between both sides of the brain. An illustration of this is the Russian composer Vissarion Shebalin who suffered two strokes in the left side of his brain. As a result he was unable to speak or to understand what words meant, however, he continued to compose music and teach music students. There are instances in medical history which demonstrate that others who have had strokes in the right side of their brain have been able to continue to compose music but have lost any feeling or emotion that they would have previously had.

Another interesting bit of brain malfunction was experienced by Maurice Ravel, the composer of that great composition, *Bolero*, who suffered from a case of brain damage in which he could "hear" music in his head but was not able to compose anymore. He progressed from constant mistakes in spelling to the point where he could not sign his name. There is no doubt that both sides of his brain were involved.

We know that when one hemisphere is damaged, frequently the opposite healthy hemisphere takes over some of the functions formerly performed by the damaged side. Whether this means that one side can fully learn to do what the other side does when the other side is no longer capable, we don't know. There are however, many case histories of persons who have demonstrated at least some ability for a healthy side of the brain to "take over" after a stroke or other brain injury has occurred. We know that some persons tend to be what we call "left brain" or "right brain", meaning that they are more analytical (left brain) or more emotionally driven (right brain). On the other hand, really good musicians need to be both left and right brain driven. Good musicians must be able to think analytically, have good timing, understand the mathematics of music, and possess many other functions that we attribute to the left brain. On the other hand, good musicians must be able to feel the music, be artistic, and possess many other functions normally attributed to the right brain. Just as many persons are ambidextrous (able to use either hand for primary functions, and both at the same time), many people are ambi-hemispherical (able to use both sides of the brain at the same time).

When "using your head and body to become a good musician", it is not important to understand everything about the "scientific" abilities or anatomy of the brain. However, it is of absolute importance to view the brain as the master conductor of *your symphony*. Your symphony is made up of your brain, your body, your soul, your instrument, and your audience. You may think that the audience is not part of *your symphony*, but it is. The audience sends signals to you that your brain interprets and sends commands to your body to perform. The audience is always part of your comfort or discomfort, your anxiety or the lack of it. The accomplished artist always "surveys" the audience before producing the first note. The emotional and environmental "tone" is set at that point and "permission" is given by the audience for the performer to perform, and the performer "requests" the participation of the audience. The audience does not only "listen"; it *participates*. The greater the degree of participation, the less the artist is a soloist. A true *soloist* is likened to practicing alone in one's studio room. It is like reading Shakespeare and coming to a part where one of the characters is doing a "soliloquy", that is talking aloud to him/herself.

Let's talk a little about how the body works with the brain. Did you ever wonder how it is that the brain says to the little finger, "move", and the little finger moves? Or how the brain doesn't seem to say anything to the lungs, yet they continue to breathe? There are pathways of nerves that run all through the body like the electrical wires that run through a building that turn on and off lights and machinery. Some of the lights are on "automatic" timers and others have to be turned on and off manually. The lungs, the heart, hormones, and other functions of the body are on "automatic". There is an in-built "pacemaker" that causes the heart to beat regularly and it functions without you thinking about it.

41

Other parts of the body require conscious commands in order to perform deliberate movements. Take writing for instance. The brain decides what it would like to "write". It sends a message to a special part of the brain called the "motor" area of the brain. This part of the brain has already determined the number of nerve endings assigned to the arm and the hand and every part of the body that performs a movement function. The message is sent for the hand to move in a specific way. The hand moves, the eyes observe and send a message back through the brain to the same motor area so that corrections can be made or whether the movement should stop and the writing left alone. (Don't show this simplistic explanation to your science or psychology teachers, it will make them laugh – because it is not "technical science language"!).

This is only the "conscious" part of movement. There are other parts that result from other kinds of "wiring" in the body. Those other "wires" are called "autonomic". This sounds a little like "automatic" doesn't it? Well, that's the whole idea. The autonomic nervous system functions whether we want it to or not and furthermore, it functions the way our *unconscious* brain tells it to! This is where the way you feel, the amount of sleep you have had (or not had!), the food you eat, the relationships you have, and the way you feel about your instrument, your teacher, your audience, and much more come into play.

Together, the central nervous system (brain and spinal cord) and the autonomic nervous system allow us to function as a whole person. It is important to remember a few things about our nervous systems:

1. The way we are made cannot always be changed, but much can be overcome. Some people seem to be "by nature" of a more "nervous temperament" than others. They also can succeed but it may require much more attention be paid to learning how to relax, gain self-confidence, and learning how to "take charge" of their nervousness. It is sometimes necessary to overcome our in-born tendencies rather than attempting to change them. Practicing correctly is the answer.

2. The central nervous system, which is composed of the brain and the nerve tracts that run up and down the spine, provide the muscle coordination, physical body balance, the breath, and the

physical dexterity and all of the other physical requirements needed to play a musical instrument.

3. The autonomic nervous system (the "automatic" part of us) operates because we tell it to do so but don't know we are telling it anything at all. This means that we must think the correct thoughts and allow self-confidence to come from deep inside us so that we will automatically function optimally.

4. Our nervous systems, particularly the autonomic (automatic) system, can be a friend. If we have trained our thinking rightly, it will come to our rescue when our conscious mind is confused.

5. The synchronous nature of our body and mind allow the central nervous system and the autonomic nervous system to work together with each overcoming the other at various times. That which "overcomes" tends to be the part that we have encouraged by rigorous and repeated practice.

Let's talk about the body's part in music. The human body is a mechanical structure with muscles, bones, and organs all held inside a huge sack made up of skin. We maintain balance largely due to a section in the lower back part of our brain called the cerebellum. The arms and legs maintain a given position due to a series of muscles and bones that move very much like a block and tackle system. When one series of muscles relaxes, the opposite ones come to attention. If they all relaxed at the same time we would fall down.

The musician must pay great attention to the body. Balance, coordination, and muscle control are essential. What we call "gross" muscle control is the ability of our large muscle structures to do what we tell them to do, such as stand at attention, or to make the broad sweeping movements when conducting an orchestra. We also have "fine" muscle control that is needed for fingering the violin or the movements for playing a piano. It usually requires much more practice to teach our "fine" muscles than the "gross" ones.

As well as the cerebellum which largely controls gross balance, we have a very tiny organ deep inside the ears called the "organ of corti" which helps with fine movements, balance, and the ability for the brain to "know" where parts of the body are at all times. For instance, a pianist can close his/her eyes and still know where every finger is, and of course, the same is true for every-one in all kinds of postural situations. In fact, many musicians play with their eyes closed at various times, and this can be done because their brain knows the position of every body part and can direct them without vision.

Although our brain and various parts of our body assist with the normal movements of life, it cannot be done without practice. In fact, they are only "natural" as a result of practice. The tiny baby falls a thousand times learning to balance, and we make a million mistakes with our fingers learning the fingering on a musical instrument, before our body movements become "natural". Just think for a moment about the complicated mind/body control necessary for the violinist to bow with one hand while fingering the strings with the other, and reading music with the eyes. No wonder it requires a tremendous amount of practice for any musician to teach the brain and the body parts to be where they are supposed to be, moving like they are supposed to move, and coordinate in unison so that music can be produced!

There are several major elements of body control. The body is basically made up of three elements: anatomical structure, electrical impulses, and chemical messages. The brain is a physical, anatomical part that is put together in a particular structure. However, those structural parts cannot operate without energy. That energy is not unlike the electrical current that runs through the wires in a house. Chemicals called "neurotransmitters" carry messages from one cell to another and from one body part to another through the electrical wires called nerves.

To control our bodies takes practice. Children are not born with the ability to control their need to urinate or defecate. We all must learn that bit of social control. To learn this kind of control takes practice. We must very slowly teach our body parts and the energy flow to those parts when and how we want them to act. This is no different from teaching our body parts how and when we want them to act in front of an audience when we are performing.

There are several steps in body training:

1. We must want to be trained. As every parent knows, a child is not likely to be "potty trained" until that child decides, for whatever reason, to be trained!

2. We must at first learn a part of the total performance then gradually learn more. The "body builder" starts with small weights and increases until great strength is achieved. Dissecting performance into the smallest possible parts is helpful. We can take those very small parts, understand them, and see why they are important. Sometimes seeing the whole of anything is difficult for us. Comprehending the complete picture takes patience and daily practice.

3. We must be satisfied at first with less than perfection. Seeing progress is more important than seeing perfection. As a matter of fact, ask the professional performer which is the more difficult, learning to play or maintaining a level of perfection. There is no doubt that we will be told that "keeping it at top quality" is by far more difficult.

4. We must be willing to make many mistakes. The only way to not make mistakes is not to try.

5. We must see each note as a solo and put our whole mind and body into that note as if it were the whole piece of music. We then begin to "feel" the music in our "bones", and phrases begin to come together and pieces of music start to "tell a story".

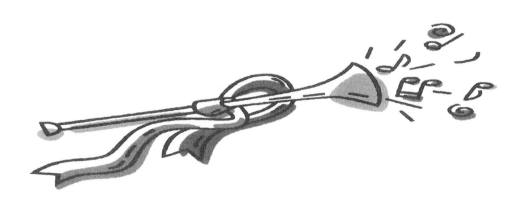

OPUS FIVE

"Although we know a great deal about the way fields affect the world as we perceive it, the truth is no one really knows what a field is. The closest we can come to describing what they are is to say that they are spatial structures in the fabric of space itself."

–Michael Talbot

"Although we do not know how music works , the truth is that no one can deny that it is the glue that holds the fabric of all things together."

–Richard H. Cox

TEN COMMANDMENTS FOR THE MUSICIAN

The commandments for the new music student are the same as those for the accomplished performer. Like other "commandments", they do not change throughout our lives. They become the basis for habit, thought process, and guides for successful performance. In this case, they refer to the person who would become and remain a fine musician.

COMMANDMENT ONE

Listen to Great Musicians of all Kinds Regularly. Since imitation is crucial to musical performance, it is imperative that we listen (and when possible, watch) great musicians at every opportunity. Listening does not mean simply "hearing" the music. It means intently listening for technique, tone, how the sound starts and stops, how the music flows from one theme to another, when and how the artist articulates each note, and other subtle factors of performance.

There was a great psychologist, Theodor Reich, who wrote a book entitled, *Listening With The Third Ear*. He helped us to see the necessity of hearing what is meant a well as what is actually said. Further, he taught us to listen to what is not said as well as that which is said. Being a psychoanalyst, trained by Sigmund Freud, Dr. Reich reached deeply into the unconscious recesses of the mind for meaning. Listening, not just hearing, is what this commandment is about. It is a matter of hearing what others miss, finding the "third dimension", and integrating it into your own brain in way that can be reproduced. Some people hear what is said. Others hear what that which is said means. Others are able to repeat what is said in a manner so that others then can hear that which the artist intended to communicate and faithfully interpret what we have heard to others. As complicated as this may sound, communication is what it is all about. We listen to be communicated *with*, and we listen so that we can communicate *with others*.

It is important that we do not limit our listening to one kind of music or to one musical instrument. Great performers borrow technique, style, musical thought, and themes from many different kinds of music. Unless we can hear the big-band behind us, it is hard to practice big-band music alone. Unless the pianist can "hear" the involvement of the symphony audience when practicing alone, it is difficult to develop the skills that communicate deep feelings when finally playing with the full orchestra. Hearing is a matter of mental concentration and identification with other performers and the audience. It is an "inside of the head" thing – close your eyes and let your brain "hear" it.

Listen to music you may not "like". If you listen carefully you may find that parts of it you do like, and further, you may discover why you do not like it and transfer that knowledge to your own performance for communication with your intended audience. Listen to music you do "like", and attempt to determine why you like it. What does it do to you? What emotions does it evoke? What bodily movements does it trigger? What memories does it recall? How can you incorporate the techniques, skills, and emotions of it into your performance?

COMMANDMENT TWO

Study with Great Teachers. Great teachers are not always great performers. Great performers are not always great teachers. Sometimes you get lucky and find a great teacher who is also a great performer, but this is the exception to the rule. Many great teachers have in the past been great performers and have turned to "passing on" their skills to the next generation.

No one can "teach" anyone else to play a musical instrument. However, great teachers can teach you to teach yourself! This is such a common mistake. Parents "take" a child to a "great teacher" and just know that the teacher can teach their child to play. Only the child can teach him/herself to play a musical instrument. The teacher can teach, demonstrate, encourage, reward, and otherwise mentor, but unless the child internalizes the information and develops a desire to play it will not work.

Many students go to lessons without "studying" how to learn to play. This is demonstrated by the rapidity with which most youngsters (and oldsters) want to immediately play songs rather than to practice scales. "Studying" how to play involves a different set of brain functions than listening and playing. Study requires attention to detail, observation of specifics of manual and mental dexterity, careful memory of processes, and a high order of mental integration.

When we have the opportunity to study with great teachers it is important that we "study" with them, not try to simply "learn how to play" from them. "Studying" includes imitating the sound, techniques and style of your teacher. It also, and maybe more importantly, includes understanding their "feeling", "emotional connection" and deep appreciation for the message the composer wanted to express.

COMMANDMENT THREE

Play and Perform at Every Opportunity. One of the most serious hindrances in learning to become a good musician is frequently the limited opportunities for performance. Performance is different than practice. Performing requires social, personal, and musical integration. Every musician rises to a higher level of musicianship when performing than when practicing. A big-band in which I played sometimes had a rather poor (I'm being kind) practice session. But since that band was made up primarily of physicians, just put that band on a bandstand in front of the State Medical Society at their annual banquet, and *voila!* Such a difference in music you never heard! The same is true in athletics. An athlete under the adrenaline rush that comes with competition, a cheering audience, and the desire to win, also experiences enhanced performance that is not there at other times. As a matter of fact, there are instances in which baseball players and runners have sprained or even broken an ankle but did not notice it until after the event was over. Such lack of knowledge is due to the brain's capacity for producing a narcotic like substance (endorphins and enkephalins) under stress that actually blocks pain. Playing under pressure is important. Playing with a cheering audience, and audiences

50

that do not cheer is important. It is important to experience as many different situations as possible so as to teach the brain and body how to react. Remember that the brain must be trained by repetition and programming, more repetition and more programming. Habit is the ability to let the programmed repetition operate with minimal conscious effort.

Children should be encouraged to play in school groups, church orchestras, small combos, and in every combination possible. Solo, duet, trio, quartet, ensemble, and every other constellation that comes along. Further, it is excellent training to perform with the "unbalanced" group. So what if there are two flutes, no drums, one saxophone, and four trombones? The sax player will learn how to blend, how to give precedence to the flute at solo time, and many other important lessons that are essential for any group playing of any kind and any place.

I can still remember playing a piano recital as a small child. I think it was not a very good performance. But the very fact that I remember it means that I learned something. Learning to control performance anxiety begins young. If a child doesn't expect it, often it never occurs. There is nothing like anticipation to make something happen, particularly negative things it seems! I also remember playing the trumpet in a marching band when it was so cold that the valves didn't want to move and mouthpiece nearly stuck to my lips. Although I cannot delineate all that I learned, I can assure you that some of that learning is still with me.

There are numerous programs for musicians to play along with musical groups, even great symphonies, by buying recordings and computer programs that do not have your particular instrument recorded. You can record yourself following the tempo, mood, and style, thus developing skills playing along with "the best of them". There is no practice like playing with persons who play better than you. It spurs you on to a higher level of musicianship every time.

COMMANDMENT FOUR

Read the Literature of Music. Learning to perform well requires much more than simply being able to play an instrument well. There is a background of knowledge that gives the performer the historical, and musical setting necessary both to perform the specific musical selection and the ability to place oneself in the proper frame of mind. When one is playing *The Star Spangled Banner*, it is important to have read the history of where it was composed, by whom, and under what conditions. Equally, it is important to identify with the burdened, work-worn slave who sang *"Ole Man River"*. No amount of playing can substitute for knowing the background of a composition, and the conditions in which music was written.

Knowing the life of the composer is equally important. The lives of John and Charles Wesley help us to know what kind of energy drove their hymnody. They were persons of very deep faith and directed their energies toward communicating a message which they felt passionately about. A study of the life of John Phillip Sousa helps us to understand how he could compose so many kinds of music ranging from operas to marches. He was a person of broad interests and extremely varied musical ability. He was not afraid to express himself in a wide range of emotional messages.

It would be most helpful for the musical student to read the lives of the great composers and analyze the factors that led them to certain kinds of music. You will find that sometimes it was national patriotism, sometimes love, sometimes religious conviction, and sometimes even anger. Study the composer, then listen to the music. See if you can hear the reason for the composition in the choice of key signature, mood, tempo, phrasing, and melody.

A study of musical literature helps us to appreciate what is behind a musical composition. Sometimes it was sheer inspiration, as in the case of *The New World Symphony*, most of the "soul songs", and many of our hymns. At other times it was the sheer demand of a new fugue to play at the cathedral on Sunday. Many of our finest composers were cathedral organists and were required to produce new compositions literally every week! The marvel is that so many of their compositions have stood the test of time, were truly great, and still exist today.

A study of the literature helps us to place ourselves within our own time, and to appreciate how the daily influences and the pressures upon us influence our inspiration and how we perform.

COMMANDMENT FIVE

Gain Confidence From Transferred Skills. The skills required for musical performance are shared with many other life activities. The good musician does not live in musical isolation. We sometimes have the mental image of the virtuoso musician as doing absolutely nothing else all day but practicing his/her chosen instrument. And, although that is sometimes the case, it is not psychologically or physically healthy. The "well-put-together" musician is one that is well rounded. This means that the piano player must learn tactile skills in other places as well as on the keyboard. This means that the wind instrument player must gain breath volume and control in other places as well as on the horn. This means that the violinist must learn poise in other places as well as with a bow and fiddle in hand.

Where do we learn other skills? The places and opportunities are multitudinous. Each person will find their own skills in many, many different activities. Dancing, typing, running, swimming, public speaking, hand-ball, tennis, sailing, roller-skating, and other physical activities are among those that help. Then there are the mental activities that offer many transferable skills. Some of the finest are foreign language study, mathematics, and other studies that require a great deal of memory. Much of our music is a combination of symbol, mathematics, translation of communication, and interpretation. These skills are transferable.

In learning theory this ability is called "transfer of training". It has been proven that a person can learn to do any one thing better if the skills required are also learned and practiced in another setting. For instance, activities that increase breathing capacity such as running will help the brass player with breathing skills that transfer from the jogging track to instrument playing. Activities that refine dexterity and motor skills transfer from practice on the computer keyboard to the piano keyboard, and vice versa. Each student will learn the specific activities that he/she enjoys and which skills are transferable to a particular instrument.

COMMANDMENT SIX

Make Sure You Have Chosen The Correct Instrument For You And Study at Least One Other Musical Instrument. Not everyone is physically (or mentally) equipped for just any instrument. You particular body-build and physical make-up is sometimes better suited for one kind of instrument and attempting to succeed on a different instrument can mean constantly working against the odds. I have a good friend who is a master pipe-organist. She discovered early in her musical education that to play the piano would require more upper body strength and longer finger reach than she had. Concentrating on the organ allowed her to excel. Not all persons have the ambidexterity for the keyboard. Some dental arrangements and lip configurations are not shaped for the clarinet. I recently worked with a young man who simply could not master the trumpet in spite of dedication and hard work. Following a careful study of his embouchure, dental formation, lip anatomy, and facial muscles, he changed to the French horn and is having remarkable success. I have seen the same kind of situation with students who were unable to master the violin, but when changed to a larger instrument (viola, cello) were quite successful. Most students choose an instrument because they like it, or because they have been influenced by someone who plays that particular instrument. However, some simply choose an instrument for unknown reasons. I have tried my best to remember why I wanted to play a trumpet, however, I cannot remember any particular reason. Some students, unfortunately, have an instrument chosen for them because a parent wants it. That is all well and good if the instrument and you fit. Just as we do not all have the same talents, we do not all have the same physical and mental make-up. We must take special care in choosing an instrument upon which we can excel and not constantly have to fight.

As with the transfer of training we discussed earlier, there is transfer of musical ability when a musician understands the requirements of another instrument. Some of us believe that the keyboard is the most essential "other instrument" to learn something about. The keyboard forces us to appreciate both the bass clef and the treble clef. It lets us visualize single notes and chords. The keyboard is truly the basis for all musical composition. In order to play any part of music well, it is necessary to "hear" the other parts. No instrument can facilitate that appreciation better than the piano keyboard. There is, in my opinion, absolutely nothing more beneficial for a musical education than at least a rudimentary knowledge of the piano. The keyboard allows us to use tactile learning to feel the keys, lets us use the ears to hear the note, lets our brain assimilate many notes at the same time into chords, and lets us see the black notes on the printed music with our eyes. The more senses we can use at any one time to learn anything, the more permanent that learning will be. We know from educational teaching methods and from studies in physiological psychology that when learning methods are compounded the result is geometric rather than simply additive. That is to say that hearing a note, seeing the note on a page of music, and playing that note is not a total of three sensations, but rather a geometric combination of each sensation with the other resulting in a more permanent learning experience.

Hearing and experiencing music played on several different instruments will also help to imprint musical knowledge in our brains. I was influenced by a high school bandmaster who believed that we should learn something about many instruments. At the time this was hard to appreciate. I had just gotten so I could play the trumpet decently when he wanted me on the French horn. I rotated from drums to mellophone, to Eb alto, to valve trombone, and eventually ended up on trumpet where I started out. Although I'm sure there are many differing opinions about such demands, it certainly does give one an appreciation for what goes into a symphonic production.

This method of "rotational learning" may not be the best for the budding virtuoso, but since most students will not become virtuosos, it is a great -

musical education. And, for the virtuoso, it is also great because the really fine performer on one instrument will without doubt continue to excel there, and also come to have a better understanding of the rest of the orchestra. Learning to play at least simple pieces on other instruments will not take you away from the instrument you love best. There is, in my opinion, absolutely nothing that can take the place of at least a rudimentary knowledge of the piano keyboard.

One of the most serious problems for conductors and musicians alike is the blending of one's instrument. Playing too loudly, too softly, and many other problems with musical expression are due to the fact that players have not learned the role of their instrument in relationship to the other instruments in the band or orchestra. Learning the rudiments of at least one other instrument helps to teach some of that understanding.

COMMANDMENT SEVEN

Study Music not just Instruments. There is a profound difference between studying music and studying a musical instrument. Learning to play an instrument even quite well does not necessarily guarantee playing music well. The knowledge of harmony, counterpoint, transposition, improvisation, composition, and much more allows one to make really great music. Also, the person who has studied conducting will have a much greater appreciation for "how music fits together" than the musician who has only played in a group. Reading a full orchestral or band score gives one a sense of "musical integration" that the solo player sometimes misses. The musician who has attempted to compose will better understand the role of chords, why we deal with consecutive fifths as we do, and the use of the octave, phrasing, and so much more.

Like in so many things in life, we are better able to be creative and innovative if we first understand the traditional foundations. I used to think that "progressive jazz" was really quite undefined, until I studied it. I then learned that it is one of the most precise of all musical modalities. Students, and performers alike, are unable to be innovative because they have not learned the basics first.

COMMANDMENT EIGHT

Place Yourself in Competition. The only thing better for the developing musician than cooperation is competition. I am not speaking of the "dog eat dog" kind of hostile environments, but rather of the "user friendly" competitions of school, state, regional, and national competitions on your instrument of choice. Competition allows for a kind of preparation unknown in other realms of musical performance. It allows for the rewards and disappointments that accompany winning and coming in second (or further down). There is nothing for musicianship growth comparable to playing in competition and with those who are more advanced than you are.

This is particularly true of single instrument competitions. It has been my privilege to be part of trumpet competitions both as performer and judge. To see the incredible preparation that young performers put into getting ready for a national competition would put many professional musicians to shame. There is nothing like playing a trumpet (or other instrument) in the midst of hundreds of other trumpeters to show you where you are in performance ability.

As it is with any skill, whether it be athletic, public speaking, debate, or music, there is no other arena in which performers can better gain both internal and external knowledge of their ability better than when in competition with others in the same field of expertise.

COMMANDMENT NINE

Learn to Play Music in Your Head. Hearing what you are going to play is important. As a matter of fact, hearing it before you play it can sometimes save considerable embarrassment. An exercise that is very helpful is to carry a small electronic tuning device with you. Then to hum the note you think the instrumentalist is playing, look at the tuning device, and see how far off you are – or if you are right on. Most persons are not blessed with "perfect pitch" (although those with it don't always see it as a blessing). Recent scientific findings indicate that almost everyone has an in-built "relative pitch". It doesn't matter, for instance, on what note of the scale a leader starts to sing, "Happy Birthday", nearly everyone can sing it. That is because we hear and perform as a result of our brain hearing and reproducing the intervals rather than the scale. This is further illustrated by the fact that most everyone can start on the same note as the leader, although they may not "know" whether the note is an "F" or a G#. Perfect pitch is not necessary for fine musicianship. Being "in tune" is! Practicing with a "tuner" is helpful since some of our ears can be fooled when listening to ourselves.

Being "in tune" is a learned ability for most people. As mentioned previously, watching a visual tuner while you practice can teach you much. It seems that some "just have it", and others never seem to acquire it. However, without being able to hear whether a note is flat or sharp will make professional musicianship difficult if not impossible. It is absolutely necessary to "hear" the note before it is produced. Learning to play or sing "in tune" takes great patience in developing hearing skills for most of us.

One of the reasons that some students have difficulty in learning to play "in tune" is because they only listen to their instrument, and at that, have not learned to accurately hear intervals. I suggest that they sit at the piano keyboard and play a note, any note, then the note above it and carefully listen, "hear it in their head", and hum the note. Then hum that note and the following note without the piano, then repeat the humming with the piano and see how close they are. I have worked with students who were nearly "tone deaf" and taught them to play at least acceptably enough to participate in school bands and orchestras. Pitch can be learned, but it takes careful and constant practice and continuous listening to oneself and any other instruments that may be around you.

Another exercise that is both fun and useful is to sing a note *before* striking the piano keyboard, then strike the note on the piano that you think you are singing. You will find that the more you practice this, the more correct you will become. At first you may be several notes off, but then as you repeat this exercise over and over, you will get closer and closer to the correct note. You can practice hearing chords and identifying them on the keyboard the same way. You can sing, the chord, then play it. Or you can play a chord then sing it.

Solfeggio and a wide variety of voice training techniques actually are very helpful for any musician in learning to "hear" and reproduce tones that are "in tune". Students who only learn instruments without voice lessons frequently miss training in vocal music, hence rarely encounter solfeggio. Solfeggio is the "do, re, mi" vocal exercises. To sing solfeggio demands a knowledge of intervals and a knowledge of the relationship of each note to the other. One of the greatest trumpet players of all time, Rafael Mendez, credits much of his success to the knowledge of solfeggio as well as the fact that his father insisted that he learn how to play many instruments.

It can also be fun to listen to the great variety of daily sounds and attempt to identify them on the keyboard by specific pitch. I have often wondered if George Gershwin got his idea for *"An American in Paris"* from that, since he imitates taxicabs, and other city sounds in that great piece of music. Just think, what note is the train whistle, what are the notes of a wailing siren, and what notes sounded in the church bell? By listening to the sixteen notes in the Westminster chime can you tell the key it is in? Try to "play" it in your head, then hit the correct notes on the piano keyboard. I remember as a small child, to manage my boredom and restlessness in church, my father would let me hold his railroad pocket watch up to my ear. Being born deaf in one ear and having lost a great deal of the hearing in the other ear, due to illness as a small child, I had a particularly keen appreciation for what I heard. I learned very early in life that I did not hear what other people said they heard. I came to recognize that the church piano would at times make a sound that was in tune with the ticking sound of my dad's watch. I could listen to the watch then wait, and sure enough before long the piano would be in tune with his watch on one note!

Hearing music in your head allows you to hear the "gestalt", i.e., the whole of the piece, before you play it. The concept of the "gestalt" has been described as the whole is greater than the sum of the parts. For instance, you can have handlebars, wheels, pedals, and a frame, but when all the parts are put together, you have a bicycle; i.e., a whole item that is greater than the sum of the parts it took to make it. The same is true in music. Each note may be beautiful, but only when many notes are put together with dynamics do you have something greater than the simple sum of a group of musical notes. You can see how the piece crescendos or fades, you can hear how you should be preparing for the next phrase while playing the current one, hence, you appreciate the whole, the gestalt.

Remember, each note is a solo. Each solo will be better if it fits with the one just played and the ones yet to come.

COMMANDMENT TEN

Practice! Practice!! Practice!!! But Practice Does Not Make Perfect!!!! There is nothing that takes the place of practice. However, both teachers and performers often do not remember that if something is practiced perfectly wrong, it will be played perfectly wrong! Correct practice leads to correct playing. Incorrect practice leads to incorrect playing. We all know both as teachers and students that it is infinitely more difficult to correct wrong habits than to learn new ones. Practice smartly!

There are also some lessons from physiological psychology that we need to remember. Items learned wrongly are sometimes remembered longer than those learned rightly. Why that should be so is a long story that is not important here, however, if I hold up a black pen and ask you to *please never* remember that it is black, you will probably never forget that it is black! There is also a law called "retroactive inhibition" that deals with our ability to remember things according to time allocation and sequence, particularly as it has to do with other matters going on in our consciousness. We learn better in small segments than in long segments. We remember better when we learn things in association with other information than in isolation. We integrate information better when we learn new information based upon already known information.

And, in truth, it is impossible to learn anything except as it is based upon and related information that you have already acquired. This is why learning the foundations of musical hearing and skill is so important. Although information learned later may be absolutely correct, it becomes incorrect when placed on top of faulty knowledge. It's the old story that tells us that it doesn't matter how well a house is built, if its foundation is sand, it will not last.

Practice cannot be substituted for anything else. But, practice using known concepts of learning can be far more beneficial than happen-chance approaches. There are no substitutes for *proper preparation.* It is true that being in the right place at the right time, good luck, and many other unknowns bring about what appears to be public success. However, success of any kind rarely comes to the unprepared.

Proper preparation includes far more than practicing on your instrument. It is necessary to practice all of the other lessons in this book as well. The whole person is the performer, not any one part. The whole person, the correct practice, the tedious patience, and the tenacious persistence, when put together produce the enjoyment of performance.

OPUS SIX

"Science affects the way we think together".
—Lewis Thomas

"Music affects the way we feel together and alone".
—Richard H. Cox

AVOIDING PERFORMANCE ANXIETY AND BUILDING PERFORMANCE CONFIDENCE

There are specific steps that can be taken to lessen performance anxiety. There are specific steps that can be taken to build performance confidence. These steps are deliberate, thought out, behavioral modifiers. Feeling "nervous" before a performance is normal. As a matter of fact, a certain amount of "concern" is probably good. I have read and heard many times that even anxiety is good. I do not agree with this at all. Concern is normal and useful. Anxiety is a physiological hindrance to good performance. When the nervous system registers "anxiety" it has already started the process of trembling, shallow breathing, rapid breathing, perspiring, and stomach discomfort. We often hear performers say that they have these symptoms until they sing or play the first note. This is not a good sign. If the physiological symptoms are present, the first note will not be at its best. Although "performance anxiety" is certainly both psychological and physiological, in the final analysis, it is the physiological elements that are the real culprits. They are things like sweating, dry mouth, shaking, goose bumps, blurred vision, and bladder demands! Both the psychology and physiology of anxiety can be greatly reduced by paying attention to the these basic steps:

Study the Baker's Dozen of lessons in this book. Don't just read them. Study them. Attempt to understand each lesson and attempt to apply each one to your particular personality and life situation. Some students come from homes with strong parental and sibling support. Others do not. In both cases, it is up to you as to how you will apply the lessons to yourself. Parental encouragement can be most beneficial, however, at other times it can be "pushy" and cause students (particularly adolescents) to rebel. Your own internal motivation is what counts -- if it is there it will come out in spite of what others say or do. However, as teachers, it is important to understand that a little encouragement often goes much further than a lot of criticism.

PREPARATION

There are three parts to all preparation, the mental, the physical and the emotional. Let us discuss each of these items one at a time.

First, let's look at mental preparation. It can be divided into five separate parts:

1. **Anticipation** – this is a matter of mind imaging. You must get a picture in your "mind's eye" of the entire situation. You can close your eyes and "visualize" the music on the page, you with your instrument, the group or accompanist with whom you are playing, and the audience. It is like creating a small picture show in the front of your brain. Think of your forehead as the picture screen on a television set. If you have a difficult time doing this, close your eyes, find a "center spot" in the middle of the inside of your forehead, and picture the entire situation as if it were a cartoon being shown frame by frame right on the front of your head.

2. **Relaxation** – the body responds to anxiety by "tightening up". The body becomes more rigid and the mind less flexible. These bodily responses are hurdles you do not need for good performance. If you have difficulty relaxing naturally, there are simple exercises that will help. Let's try one. Sit in a comfortable chair, or lie flat on a bed. Close your eyes. Breathe slowly and regularly, very deeply, and count slowly from one to ten, breathing in and out very slowly on each count. Talk to yourself. Tell yourself that with each breath you will become more and more relaxed – and behold – you will.

3. **Performing in your mind** – remember, earlier in this book I talked about the value of "hearing" it in the mind. Now we actually perform it in our mind. By going through the performance step by step we can anticipate and help to avoid surprise feelings. It is very much like anticipating the next note when we play. The best way to play the next note correctly is to anticipate how it will

65

be executed and how it will sound within the context of the last note and the next several notes.

4. **Center on the message** – remember that we are playing music to communicate. It is important to remember the message we wish to send to the audience. They will not remember the "wrong" notes nearly as much as they will remember the communication. Mental preparation takes time. We have to carefully think through just how the piece of music that we have chosen will send the desired message. Then by keeping that message in mind we can allow the actual technical performance to call upon our hours and years of practice and musical preparation. Learning the music simply by reading it, while not playing on the instrument, is sometimes helpful. Many great musicians memorize the actual music straight from the printed page in their head, while humming it, and actually doing the fingering manually but not at the keyboard. Then they put it all together in their mind, then on the instrument.

5. **Center yourself** – get in touch with your own emotions. If you are preoccupied, the music will show it. It is absolutely necessary to "get lost" in the music, otherwise you become a showperson, not a musician. A technique that was discussed earlier will also help here. Close your eyes briefly, and with your eyes closed, let your eyes "center" on an imaginary spot in the center of your forehead. This method of "talking to yourself" allows your to "center" your thoughts. Then "center" your body. Stand in a comfortable position (if you are standing), or adjust your legs, buttocks, back, neck and head in a comfortable position (if you are sitting). Balancing your body is extremely important at or with your instrument. At the keyboard it is important not to have to stress your reach or feel awkward in your movements. When playing a wind instrument, it is extremely important to balance your body with the weight and feel of the instrument as part of your whole body posture. Some young musicians see unusual

eccentricities, contortions, and very incorrect postures used by "professionals" and attempt to copy them. Each of us seem to develop enough of our own strange habits without copying any-one else's! You can get in touch with yourself at the same time that you practice the relaxation exercises. It is usually helpful to be in a totally quiet place and allow yourself the luxury of deep meditation. During this process you can dedicate yourself to the purpose of your performance, not only to the correctness of it. This aspect of mental preparation requires whole brain activity. By that we mean that you are keenly aware of the intellectual demands upon you, the emotional demands upon you, and the alertness yet confidence you have stored up during your hours and days of practice. Meditation as a daily exercise is very help-ful for your whole person, not just for your musical performance. Fifteen minutes of meditation with relaxation twice daily is a tonic that cannot be equaled by any known medicine!

The next step is physical preparation. There are also several distinct parts to this kind of preparation:

1. **General health** – poor physical health is a hindrance to perform-ing well. Keeping one's body in tone, weight within normal limits, bodily functions within normal, and moderate exercise, all are essential for the best performance. After all, the instrument is only an extension of your inner self. If you feel well physically, you will doubtless communicate better than if you are feeling ill. It is surprising how many musicians abuse their bodies with inadequate exercise, too much caffeine, alcohol, tobacco, illegal and prescription drugs, and overweight.

2. **Nutrition** – someone has said that we are what we eat. They are probably right. Further, food plays a far more important role in good performance than most musicians want to acknowledge. Too much sugar, excessive caffeine, and excess fats, are only a few of the things to avoid. If alcohol can impair one's driving, guess what it can do to one's musical performance! Regularity of

eating is frequently difficult for professional musicians due to performance times, travel, and other scheduling problems. However, it is important to keep one's blood sugar level under control and within normal limits at all times. "Sugar highs" are artificial and often run out during a performance, just like alcohol "highs" often become withdrawal "lows". Caffeine, tobacco, and alcohol are no doubt the nemesis of many performers. Most stimulants are in the long-run depressants and are not needed.

3. **Sleep** – the loss of sleep produces serious effects. We tend to see only the tiredness that results. In fact, the tiredness is only a symptom of the real problem, dream deprivation. Dreams are essential for the repair of our entire thought process system. There have been many experiments where persons were not allowed to dream. These people became extremely tired and talked and acted as if they were mentally ill. Natural sleep has several different phases. When we do not sleep regularly, we develop sleep habits that skip important phases of sleep. One of these phases is the stage in which we dream. Dreaming seems to restore the brain and create energy for the next period of wakefulness. Regular hours of sleep are often very difficult for the traveling performer. It is particularly difficult to obtain enough sleep before midnight. Research has shown that one hour of sleep before midnight is worth two hours after midnight. Most nighttime performers play into the wee hours and suffer from sleep deprivation. Some folks who don't maintain regular sleep hours turn to medication and drugs to help them. Sleep that comes as a result of chemicals is not natural and does not produce the same beneficial results. When someone says, "I took a sleeping pill and slept like a rock", usually also is admitting that they did not dream. When this becomes a habit, they have a serious problem.

4. **Medicines** – all medicines are drugs and have both beneficial and harmful effects. A prescription medicine, Inderal™ (propranolol hydrochloride) has become fashionable among some musicians

68

to control stage fright. This medicine (and others like it), work because they are "Beta blockers", i.e. they block certain impulses to the heart. This is a medicine that has profound effects upon the heart and the nervous system that controls the entire cardiovascular system. Do yourself a favor and talk with your doctor or pharmacist before starting what could become a dangerous habit. Be sure and ask to read the "side effects" of any medicine you take, whether prescription or over-the-counter. Anytime you take medicine make sure you know the "side effects". Some medicines dry you out (diuretics), some make you drowsy (antihistamines), some make you jittery (some cold and flu medicines), some cause nausea (some antibiotics), some produce diarrhea, some keep you awake, and there are thousands of other effects you need to take into account when taking medicine. Another very serious problem with relying upon medications for stage confidence is that like all medications, they tend to become habit forming, sometimes psychologically and sometimes both physically and psychologically. They also not infrequently lead to heavier doses, more powerful medications, and additive chemical substances such as alcohol and nicotine – both of which have profound effects upon heart rate, breathing, and nervous system functioning.

5. **Doctors and Dentists** – Be sure your doctor or dentist knows that you are a musician and understands that treatments and medications can effect your ability to study and perform. When undergoing surgery, if at all possible request "local" anesthetic. General anesthesia puts the nervous system of the whole body to sleep – that's why they can operate on your foot or your head without your feeling it. It usually requires considerably more time to "bounce back" from general anesthesia than from local anesthetics and the complications can be severe. I have personally worked with musicians who required a considerable period of time following general anesthesia to regain the full and finely

tuned motor coordination they had enjoyed prior to surgery. If you are a wind instrument player remind your dentist that your lips need to be treated gently. Not all persons who work on your body understand clearly enough how even small changes in tooth structure, muscular ability, dry mouth, and a myriad of other things can effect your musical ability. They won't know you are a musician unless you tell them and let them know how the part they may be working on could effect your playing. Invite your health care providers into your life and let them help you with your overall health and help you protect your functions as much as possible when illness occurs.

6. **Your brain** – it is actually two! Well, maybe not two whole brains, but two sides that can work separately or together with each other. We have already talked a lot about this topic. But, a review of this important aspect of managing your head and body needs to be done. The two sides of our brain are called "hemispheres". Each side has peculiarities that are important to understand, particularly for the musician. There is the left hemisphere, or side, and the right hemisphere. The left side of the brain is known for its analytical functions. The kinds of things that are needed for putting the technical aspects of playing together are in this part. This side of the brain is best prepared by mastery of many subjects, not just music. Mathematics, science, and other analytical and technical studies will help prepare this side of the brain. The left side of the brain is where we have logic and order. Sometimes I think of the left brain as the "marching band" side and the right brain as the "symphony side". Right brain activity is the emotive, the artistic, the romantic, and the creative aspects of the brain. Studying music appreciation – not just technical production- learning to truly listen to and appreciate what music does to the psyche and the soul is important to the right side of the brain. Learning how to paint, appreciate nature, enjoy works

of art, create poems, write stories, and anything else you can think of that is creative will help develop this side of the brain.

7. **The Whole Brain** – There is a structure in the brain called the "corpus callosum". (Remember this from earlier reading? – another review!). It is extremely important because it serves as the great switchboard that connects the left side and the right side of the brain together. This is where your brain does the balancing act and puts the logic and analytical part of the left brain together with the artistic and creative right side. When the brain is functioning as a whole, you are in a great place to artistically perform yet with correct technique.

8. **The Whole Person** – The concept of a "whole person" seems strange and difficult to understand for many persons. The concept of "wholeness" or holistic thinking encompasses the mind, the body, and the spirit. It includes what we think, what we do, how we feel, what we believe, how we feel about ourselves, how we relate to others, and thousands of other aspects of our total being. Even thought the concept of the whole person seems rather esoteric at first, until we grasp the concept and see how we individually fit into it. We cannot appreciate the role of music in everyday life, our role as musicians in other person's lives, and the totality of the life we live until we experience the meaning of the whole person. Our mind, body, and spirit are at the same time distinctly separate and yet distinctly together. They function in harmony whether we wish them to do so or not. What we think is how we act, and how we think and act represents the spirit within us. Once we grasp the concept of the whole person and are able to embrace it, it is amazing how much easier it is to communicate with others and to allow our music to touch the lives of others.

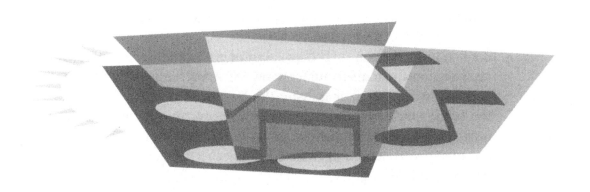

IT'S SHOW TIME !

OPUS SEVEN

"For everything there is a season." –Ecclesiastes

"There is a season for study, a season for practice, and then – there is show time!"
–Richard H. Cox

The ultimate "proof of the pudding" for the musician is show time. Our hours of study, preparation, practice, and anticipation all come together sometimes for only a few minutes. Each breath you take reveals your physiological control, each step you take demonstrates your self-confidence, and each note you play becomes a solo indeed.

There are always judges present. Sometimes those judges are rating you in a competition, sometimes they are listening to you audition, sometimes they are the audience, and sometimes "they" are only you. But they are always there. We have all heard from time to time that we are our own worst critic. This is both good and bad. Being a good critic of ourselves is essential. We cannot allow ourselves to become sloppy or undisciplined. The problem comes in that we apologize for our lack of practice and discipline. When that occurs, we need to be our own worst critic. When we have practiced faithfully, disciplined ourselves to the best of our ability, and sincerely attempted to do our very best, it is important to give ourselves credit. We need to stand erect, hold our head high, and walk out on that stage with the full confidence that a practiced and disciplined musician's life demands and deserves!

Now, how do we get ready for show time? This book has outlined for you a step by step field guide that when put into practice will prepare you to "face the music"! It will be helpful to take one lesson per day and think about it. Mull it over. Even if it sounds like something you have heard before – remember that remembering is repetition. Talk to your musician friends about the lesson, ask your music teachers what they think, and most of all believe the lesson unless you can prove that it is untrue. Sometimes trying to prove something is not true helps us to "process" it in our minds and actually come to find out that it is true.

These thirteen easy lessons help us to think correctly. Good musicianship and professional playing is far more how and what we think than most music teachers emphasize. When we remember that *we* are the instrument and that the horn or piano is simply our speaker system, it is easier to understand that our thinking is where everything we want to communicate starts.

Next, it is essential to understand that when perform we use not only our own symbols and rituals, but also appeal to whatever meaning the audience has attached to those symbols and rituals. Music provides some of the most powerful symbols known to humankind. Remember that most people stand when they hear the national anthem and many cry when they hear "taps" at a funeral. This is because we are conditioned to respond to symbols and rituals. As you prepare your music it is important to keep in mind what message you want to give them and what symbols and rituals you will employ to accomplish that end.

As we prepare and move toward that show time moment, we must practice the art of transcendence on a daily basis. We learn to become greater than we are by growing in self-confidence and humility at the same time. We bond with our instrument, allow it to speak for us, and overcome our weaknesses by superceding our fears and weaknesses with a message that we simply must deliver. We transcend the moment by allowing our communication to be so important that petty circumstances cannot interfere.

Keeping the body and the brain in shape is no small task. It cannot be done by only practicing on our instrument. It takes exercise, a healthy diet, healthy thought processes, positive friendships, a depth of personal spirituality, and plenty of sleep. It also demands that we stay away from excesses of all kinds, particularly those that include medications, caffeine, tobacco, and alcohol.

Then there are the commandments listed in this book. Like all commandments, they must be regarded as more than mere suggestions. We must take them to heart and seriously attempt to observe them. A careful study of the "Ten Commandments for Musicians" listed in this book show that when taken together they have to do with far more than simply playing an instrument. Our person is the instrument and the commandments allow us to develop ourselves into a mighty messenger. We then pick up our horn or sit at the keyboard and allow it to magnify and amplify our message.

There is a careful balance between self-confidence and over-confidence when it comes to show time. The self-confidence that comes from careful and persistent preparation is not arrogance. True humility is not self-castigation. Both self-confidence and humility come from combining ones gifts with determination and endurance. When show time arrives it is possible to be proud without arrogance. It is possible to be confident without being egotistical. It is possible to be humble without being a doormat. It is showtime – you are ready -- just do it!

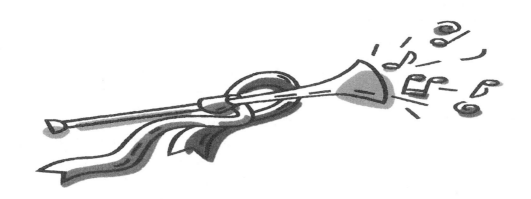

POSTLUDE

This book has been offered as a *help*. It does not provide *answers*. The purpose of teaching is to encourage others to think and to arrive at their own individual answers to their own unique challenges. As a teacher, I have always felt that if after delivering an address, a lesson, or a workshop that if I had not raised more questions than I answered, it was not successful teaching. There is probably no other human activity that demands any more originality and individual uniqueness than musical performance. It takes years to develop an individual "style". Although "style" can be imitated, it cannot be copied because it is deeply imbedded in the unique mind, body physique, mental set, belief system, and ego of the performer. Answers for one person only raise questions for another. This is why it is impossible to "teach someone to play" an instrument. A good teacher can model, instruct, offer suggestions, explain technique, and many other things, but in the final analysis, only the student can teach him/herself to play! As master teachers, we teach others how to teach themselves. Hopefully, we teach them how to become whole persons who use every ounce of their being to communicate wholeness to others.

Communication without a message is a waste of time. Musical expression without a message is simply technology the technology of sound. Musical expression with a message is an art form that transcends both sound and technology and moves the human soul to a spiritual level.

Learning music is incredibly an individual, personal journey. Although there may be others on a similar road, you are the only one on that particular road. Although others learning the same or different instruments can beneficially share their experiences, yours will always be uniquely your own. Although others will think they know how you feel, they will not. Although others will encourage you, the only true encouragement will come from within you as a result of your private relationship with your instrument, the music, and those who have given so much of themselves so you can be you.

SELECTED READINGS

General Reading:

Ayers, A. Jean, *Sensory Integration and the Child.* Los Angeles: Western Psychological Services, 1979

Bono, E. de, *Children Solve Problems.* New York: Harper and Row, 1974

Campbell, Don G., *Introduction to the Musical Brain, 2nd Edition.* MMB Music, St. Louis, 1992

Gardner, Howard, *The Arts and Human Development: A Psychological Study of the Artistic Process.* New York: John Wiley and Sons, 1973

Schneiderman, Barbara, *Confident Music Performance.* MMB Music, St. Louis, 1992

Specialized Reading:

Blacking, J., *How Musical Is Man?* University of Washington Press, Seattle, 1973

Corballis, M.C., *Neuropsychology of perceptual functions; in Zaidel (Ed.), Neuropsychology: Handbook of Perception and Cognition.* Academic Press, San Diego, 1995

Deutsch, Diana, Ed., *The Psychology of Music, 2nd Edition.* New York, 1999

Goode, Michael I., *Stage Fright in Music Performance and its Relationship to the Unconscious.* Second Edition., Trumpetworks Press, Oak Park, IL 60301

Horvath, Janet, *Playing (less)Hurt: An Injury Prevention Guide for Musicians,* 2400 Hennepin Dr., Minneapolis, MN 55405

Knoblauch, Steven H., *The Musical Edge of Therapeutic Dialogue,* Analytic Press, Hillsdale, NJ, 2000

Lucinda-Lewis, *Broken Embouchures*, An Embouchure Handbook and Repair Guide (for brass players), Oscar's House Publishing, NJ, 2002

Rossing, T.D., *The Science of Sound, 2nd Edition.* Addison-Wesley, New York, 1990

Spintge, Ralph and Droh, Roland, (Eds.), *Music Medicine,* NMB Music, Inc., St. Louis, MO, 1992

Elkin, Ida, *Technical Work in Ear Training and Sight Reading*, Carl Fischer, Chicago 1955 (this is a piano book and can be used by most instruments with benefit).

HIGHLY RECOMMENDED RESOURCES FOR YOUNG (and old) MUSICIANS*

This list is intended as a "user-friendly" list – not at all exhaustive – but resources that have been particularly helpful to me and persons with whom I have worked over the years. Many of them tend to be "brass-player" oriented since that has been my major area of musical participation in recent years. The web should be browsed for organizations that specialize in individual instruments such as trombones, saxophones, etc. similar to the International Trumpet Guild and the National Trumpet Competition.

In addition to the following listings, the Author of this book, Dr. Richard H. Cox is available for workshops, clinics, and private confidential consultation. Email: r-bcox@ix.netcom.com or by phone: 719/632-5653

smartmusic®

Students practice more, build skills, and gain confidence with SmartMusic. The SmartMusic system listens to students sing or play through a microphone attached to a computer. With accompaniments for over 30,000 titles, students practice their individual part while listening to the piece as a whole. They see – and hear – immediate feedback on how well they're doing. www.smartmusic.com

finale®

Already the world's premiere music notation software, Finale 2006 raises the bar with even more power and speed, revolutionary tools for teaching composition and arranging, and professional-quality Garritan sounds.

Music Education Madness (particularly the "Music Education Resource Directory". www.musiceducationmadness.com

ChopSaver

"For musicians with lips" – the finest of natural products compounded by professionals. The finest product this author has found for chapped, over-tired, abused, and irritated lips. Developed by a trumpet player and now widely accepted as the best product on the market for lip-care. www.chopsaver.com

Dillon's Music

"First in classic brass. Recognized as one of the finest resources for musical instruments and accessories. New and used as well as expert instrument repair". 325 Fulton St., Woodbridge, NJ 07095, 732/634-3399, www.dillonmusic.com. Offering the Brass World, the largest selection of new & used instruments on the web. From major brands to the more obscure, you can find them all at Dillon Music.

The Association of Concert Bands

This is an important organization for every band instrument musician to know about. Since the majority of persons who learn to play instruments will look for opportunities to continue their musical interests following high school and college (many while they pursue other professional lines of work) this organization promotes community bands. Those in community bands are urged to contact this organization for information, membership and opportunities for excellence in musicianship. www.acbands.org

The Midwest Clinic

"The Midwest Clinic exists for educational purposes exclusively; to raise the standards of music education; to improve the methods employed in music education; to develop new teaching techniques; to disseminate to school music teachers, directors, supervisors and others interested in music education information to assist in their professional work; to examine, analyze and appraise

literature dealing with music; to hold clinics, lectures, and demonstrations for the betterment of music education; and in general, to assist teachers and others interested in music education in better pursuing their profession". This is a most prestigious organization that provides an annual convention held in Chicago, Illinois each December. The Clinic attracts literally thousands of musical performers, composers, conductors, educators as well as exhibitors of every conceivable product for musical education and performance.

Contact: Kelly Jocius, Executive Administrator, The Midwest Clinic
828 Davis St., Ste. 100, Evanston, Illinois 600201 USA
Phone: (001)847-424-5185

Power Lung Products

An essential piece of equipment for musicians, particularly voice and wind instrument players. *"Breathing for performing artists".* It is the only breathing assistance device that I know of which has amassed supporting evidence from independent studies proving its effectiveness. The author of this book highly recommends it for voice and instrumental musicians alike. It is well worthwhile for sports enthusiasts as well. www.powerlung.com. 800/ 903-3087 or 713/465-1180

The Instrumentalist Magazine

An important source of information and articles of interest to musicians, young and old alike. Up-to-date as well as marvelous historical data to enrich the curious musical mind. Articles are written by persons with many years experience and offer a wealth of information for persons who wish to learn more and keep current in music. Regular reading of a publication such as this "feeds" a growing musical mind. www.instrumentalist.com

The National Trumpet Competition

"NTC was founded in 1991 and has hosted nearly 4,000 of the nation's youngest trumpet players as they strive to gain experience and recognition. NTC has been instrumental in providing performing and educational opportunities for young and developing players. An annul convention and competition

is offered and a most rewarding experience awaits those who attend, from individual consultation with performance experts, clinics, group playing, and listening to premier trumpeters and musical groups from around the world".
 Contact: Dr. Dennis Edelbrock, George Mason University, Fairfax, VA
www.nationaltrumpetcomp.org

The International Trumpet Guild

Provides a wonderful journal and annual conventions as well as opportunities for young trumpet players to compete and perform. Contact: ITG, 241 East Main Street, #247, Westfield, MA 01086-1633, www.trumpetguild.org

Robert King Music Sales
140 Main St., North Easton, MA 02356
Email: commerce@rkingmusic.com www.kingmusic.com
An excellent resource for an incredibly wide selection of music for all instruments and all occasions.

Interlochen Center for the Arts

Interlochen, MI. An internationally known resource for young musicians. Year round and summer programs with internationally renown instructors, numerous opportunities for individual and group
participation and performance. Many of the top professional players of the day are graduates of Interlochen. Contact: Dr. Michael Albaugh, Director of Music, www.interlochen.org

The Performing Arts Medicine Association
"A professional organization that specializes in the understanding and assistance to musicians who have medical challenges as well as education and conferences to enhance knowledge in the field of medical concerns relating to musicians". www.artsmed.org

Warburton Music Products

Manufacturers of quality brass instrument mouth-pieces since 1974. *"Dr. Cox the author performs using Warburton mouthpieces."*

Contact: Bruce Gordon, P.O. Box 1209, Geneva, FL 32732. 1-800-638-1950
www.warburton-usa.com

NOTE: These listings are not the only resources in any given area, however, they have been found particularly valuable by the author of this book. Students have benefited from these resources in positive predictable ways. No specific claims are made by this listing in terms of correcting any problem area or any guaranteed outcome. Persons with medical and/or psychological concerns are urged to seek appropriate professional consultation.

Made in the USA
Middletown, DE
30 April 2019